I0821788

Praise for *Finding Peace When a Child Chooses Another Path*

"Few of us are untouched by the pain of loved ones taking other paths than the one we would choose for them. Robin Baker provides a thoughtful and practical guide for loving our way through the high cost of agency."

—Terryl Givens, professor of literature and religion at the University of Richmond; author of *The Crucible of Doubt* and *The God Who Weeps*

"Parents scarcely know what to do when a child leaves the Church. How can they explain the departure? Is it the parents' fault? What can be done to get the son or daughter back? How can parents show love when they are feeling so much pain? Robin Baker has collected the experiences of Latter-day Saint parents who have gone through this arduous trial and to these added information about relevant religious trends. Her informal, candid, and lively account will help parents think more clearly about what is happening and how to respond."

—Richard Bushman, author of *Joseph Smith: Rough Stone Rolling*

"After finding herself among the 'invisible group' with wandering children, Robin Baker set out to come to terms with a new, unexpected version of her life. This helpful book offers wisdom and hope gleaned during the process, along with the recognition that these stories are not over yet."

—Claudia L. Bushman, author of *Contemporary Mormonism*

"When young adults journey away from the LDS faith, their parents begin a journey of their own—a journey rife with self-examination, prayerful pleading, and adjustments of many kinds. Robin's personal stories, and those of others she has interviewed, help parents better imagine the territory ahead so as to approach this journey with not only hope but humility, perspective, and great love. Honest, compassionate, and wise, Robin's voice rings true and clear."

—Wendy Ulrich, PhD; author of *Weakness Is Not Sin* and *The Temple Experience*

FINDING *peace*

WHEN A CHILD CHOOSES ANOTHER PATH

WHEN A CHILD
CHOOSES
ANOTHER PATH

ROBIN ZENGER BAKER

CFI
An Imprint of Cedar Fort, Inc.
Springville, Utah

ISBN 13: 978-1-4621-1647-8

Published by CFI, an imprint of Cedar Fort, Inc.
2373 W. 700 S., Springville, UT 84663
Distributed by Cedar Fort, Inc., www.cedarfort.com

LIBRARY OF CONGRESS CATALOGING-IN-PUBLICATION DATA

Baker, Robin Zenger, 1957- author.
Finding peace when a child chooses another path / Robin Zenger Baker.
pages cm
Includes bibliographical references.
ISBN 978-1-4621-1647-8 (perfect bound : alk. paper)
1. Mormon youth--Religious life. 2. Church attendance. 3. Ex-church members--Church of Jesus Christ of Latter-day Saints. I. Title.

BX8643.Y6B35 2015
248.8'45--dc23

2015015956

Cover design by Shawnda T. Craig

Edited and typeset by Kevin Haws

Printed in the United States of America

10 9 8 7 6 5 4 3 2 1

Printed on acid-free paper

Dedication

To Shannon, Scott, Leslie, and Kelly, who continue to teach me many wonderful life lessons.

To my parents, whose dedication to making a contribution to the world was contagious.

To my husband, Rich, for his unflagging support through every phase of this project.

Contents

Introduction

In a recent LDS Sunday School class, the teacher queried, "How many of us have a close family member or loved one who no longer believes in the Church or has quit coming?" Nearly every hand in the room went up.

It seems that if we do not personally know someone close to us who has left our religion behind, we at least know someone who *is* facing this situation. If you are reading this book, perhaps this has happened in your circle of loved ones. If not, you may be wondering whether "there but for the grace of God go I." It can be difficult for parents to watch their beloved children turn away from cherished beliefs. Parents may question their childrearing and feel guilty for past mistakes. They may wish they had done things a different way, and certainly wish things had *turned out* different. As one parent of a departing teen described, "I just wanted to wake up and have everything be like it used to be."

One of the most beautiful phrases in the Book of Mormon affirms, "Men are, that they might have joy" (2 Nephi 2:25). We know that this life has the potential to bring us many good things, including close family, a healthy relationship with God, the assurance that children have learned important life lessons, and the peace of a life well lived. But watching children take another path sends parents into uncharted territory, feeling alone, frustrated, and unsure where to turn for understanding and guidance. There are new worries about the long-term future of the child and about the family. Parents may feel anger, bitterness, or guilt. They may *want* to feel acceptance and gratitude toward all of their life circumstances, but find this goal elusive.

Even though parents cannot pick their child's path, they can pick their response. As the mother of several children who have chosen paths outside the gospel, I have felt firsthand the emotional toll of having children step away from the gospel path. I quickly discovered that I had become part of a large but surprisingly invisible group of people. I recognized there were many people in my congregation, family, and circle of friends who have loved ones outside of the Church, but because people did not talk much about this subject, I didn't know much about their journeys. I believed there was a possible happy way to live this new life trajectory but that I still had a lot to learn about how to make it happen. I quickly learned that talking to other parents in the same situation was extremely helpful. I knew there was a great deal of collective wisdom out there from other parents of departing children, so I began to interview people, asking them to share their solutions for finding peace. I found so much help from this that I began to write about what I was learning. This book is an attempt to share this collective wisdom with other parents in my shoes.

Our Family Experience

When I was a young mother, I naïvely believed that parenting would not be all that hard. I tackled the challenge with gusto and read constantly on the topic of childrearing. I assumed I would do most everything right. I would be patient, loving, spiritual, and fun. My children would set the gold standard for kindness, braininess, athletic ability, and musical prowess. Of course, they would love the Church and gospel as I had as a child and young missionary. I was going to do everything in my power to help them be fully converted and feel those warm, lovely feelings I got every time I went to Church or performed service.

But my children started growing up. I quickly grew to appreciate that I was swimming upstream, and these children came with their own prickly or sweet personalities. I loved them all, but some were easier than others to raise. One of my children pushed every boundary; we joked that she ran full steam ahead toward every metaphorical brick wall around her. When we watched a Church movie about an alcoholic who later reformed so he could raise his orphaned niece, she quizzed me about what alcohol was and how it felt to drink it. She was only eight at the time, and her conclusion was, "I want to try that."

My other children were less adventurous but no less challenging. Another daughter wanted to do every single thing right and would often consult me when she needed to make any decision, large or small. At four, she would remind *me* to make sure we all brushed our teeth before we left the house. She taught herself to tie her own shoes, read, and play the piano. Her conscientiousness was legendary, and nothing short of perfection would do.

But at this moment, these two beautiful daughters have left the Church. Our family currently has two in and two mostly out. Our oldest says she still believes in God and is not sorry she was raised Mormon. Our younger daughter has not ruled out returning to the faith someday, but neither of them currently attends under their own steam. And this is painful for me. My two daughters' departures from the Church have profoundly impacted me, though in different ways.

Our one daughter's exit from the Church started early, maybe at birth. All her life, she seemed to seek out mischief, or perhaps it just found her. She was an adorable, fun-loving girl, and all kinds of people enjoyed being with her, including those who got into trouble. When she was a teen, she had been grounded multiple times, suspended from school, and knew the local police officers on a first-name basis. She wanted to quit coming to church, but we required her to attend *some* church, even if it was not ours. She thought she might like to be Catholic like her friends, but the local Catholic congregation had no mechanism to teach her about their beliefs, so during high school, she eventually returned to our LDS congregation and helped teach Primary.

As her mother, I was stressed and sad about her actions, but when she reached eighteen, it was honestly something of a relief when I no longer felt quite so responsible for getting her to church each week. At that point, it was clearly her decision whether she wanted to live an LDS lifestyle and be part of the community of Saints where we lived. For her, we recognized early that remaining in the Church was perhaps unlikely.

My younger daughter—the one who wanted to do everything perfectly—was a different story. When she went off to college, we knew there was a chance she would stop attending church. She had never been particularly gung-ho about her early morning seminary class, but she hadn't been rebellious either. She was just a bright, thoughtful, regular teenage girl with normal impulses to fit in, have fun, and get enough sleep—so she didn't particularly jump at the chance to attend seminary at 6:30 a.m. In fact, she was quite late most days, as she was burning the candle at both ends, staying up until the wee hours to do well academically. Neither did she develop any special commitment to scripture reading or personal prayer during high school. She finished her Young Women's Personal Progress goals under duress, but I didn't worry about her because she didn't drink or smoke or do drugs, and she bore her testimony occasionally and she never fought us on church attendance or on the rule of waiting until sixteen to date. She was a strong student, and school was her first priority.

To help maximize her chances of staying active, we encouraged her to attend a Church university, which she did for two years. She had good experiences there; she found friends, joined a singing group, excelled in school, won awards, and liked her roommate and most of her classes and teachers. She just did not enjoy church. She flew under the radar and got involved only superficially. She served in a few small ways by teaching a Sunday School lesson, playing the piano in sacrament meeting once, and doing her visiting teaching with her roommate, but she was never asked to speak in church and never held a calling that required much time or effort.

She seemed fully capable of handling her problems on her own and didn't seek out or find her own pipeline to God through her own spiritual longings, and nothing seemed amiss to her. Nothing seemed amiss to us either, and we didn't worry about her too much. She didn't read scriptures on her own, and we guessed she might not be praying much either. She tended to be more interested in her phone than the talks during church, but that seemed typical for her age group. She was doing most things right, but for whatever reason she simply lacked a passion for spiritual things.

After a few years of college, she decided to leave BYU. We were pleased when she chose to attend a university in Utah, in a predominately LDS environment. We felt this would leave open the possibility that she would find a fantastic, thoughtful, strong religious environment in the LDS faith, and therefore finally find her religious niche within the Church. She moved to another city within Utah, but she never found that congregation.

After her move, I called her every Sunday to ask if she had made it to church, but she was always sleeping in, or hadn't figured out which ward was hers, or had other things to do—mostly sleeping. She had no LDS roommates or friends in her new city and didn't know anyone in the ward. She didn't want to try to find her ward. Every Sunday morning, I would call her and let the phone ring. And ring. And ring. And every Sunday I felt devastated, as I worried she wasn't where she needed to be. What was she missing? What was she doing? Would she ever return if she left? Was she getting into trouble?

I prayed hard. I tried to think of everything I could possibly do to help her from afar. I encouraged her sister to visit and take her to church. But she lived far away and had her own life and responsibilities. I called her old roommate and asked for her help, but I got a lukewarm response. We obtained two tickets to general conference, but she wasn't enthusiastic to go, and she and her sister missed the meeting. I called her bishop and begged him to do something. He said he would do what he could, but that there were quite a few just like her on their rolls.

One day, all the stars aligned and my other daughter and I visited her on a Sunday when her ward was in session. She was willing to go and, as luck would have it, it turned out to be a week where the bishop randomly picked people out of the audience to speak impromptu. I was a little shocked when my daughter's name was chosen, and she stood up confidently to share her feelings of love for her sister.

It was a sweet but short-lived success. The other talks given that day were remarkable; the thoughtfulness and faithfulness present among those who were in her ward were impressive. One young man shared quotes from a talk by Terryl Givens called "Letter to a Doubter," which felt like a gift had just been handed to both of us. I felt some hope that she would see the value of her congregation. My daughter agreed that she lived in a fantastic ward, but she never returned.

Instead, she began experimenting with her hair, makeup, and clothing to look a bit less like a sweet Mormon girl and a little more cosmopolitan and edgy. She left off following Church guidelines. She found a new boyfriend, who had likewise stopped going to church after leaving BYU. He was kind, funny, smart, talented, and completely likeable. And he too no longer followed Church rules, had grown his hair long, and felt ambivalent towards the gospel.

Back in Boston, I found Sundays the most difficult day of the week. I worried about this daughter constantly and pondered what I could say or write to her. I wondered if I couldn't be the right one to say the right thing, who could? It was a miserable time, and I just could not accept that this was happening. People assured me she would eventually come around, but I knew as well as anyone that the longer she was out, the less chance that would happen. There were certainly no guarantees, and I recognized this was not something I could control. I was devastated and felt like a failure as a parent. I wanted to blame others, but I knew that was completely unhelpful. I had no idea what to do and how to feel better.

But I knew I had at least some control over how I responded to this new reality in our family. I could curl into myself and hide, or I could go public. I could complain to my friends and whine to complete strangers, or keep this a secret. I chose to broadcast my woes. This topic was always on my mind, so out of my mouth it came. The funny thing was that I did start to feel better. Others' thoughts on the topic were healing to me. Some of them had been through similar experiences and shared ideas that had helped them find hope and peace. As I kept talking to people, I realized that there was a lot of collective wisdom out there. If these ideas were working for me, perhaps they would work for others.

So I decided to do some research. I decided to be more systematic in discovering how other people had dealt with similar experiences of children leaving the Church. I knew that others wiser than I had figured out some secrets to surviving, and even thriving in this situation. Even though I knew it would be difficult for people to talk about their personal sorrows, I felt it could greatly help others to hear some of these insights and feel some camaraderie. It was also something active I could do to beat back my own sadness.

My goal in doing this was not to come up with the one and only true way everyone should handle the faith transitions of their loved ones. Just as every story is unique, so too solutions must be tailored to the circumstances and personalities of those involved. Instead, I wanted to present an array of experiences and perspectives that had actually worked for people, so that, out of this smorgasbord of wisdom, others might find something they could use to help salve their wounds and better cope with their feelings. I wanted people to feel less alone, and I believed that these stories mattered.

There was just one problem: I had to get people to go on record to share their stories. This was not easy. These were difficult stories to tell. Not everyone was willing to talk. Some were afraid of offending or betraying their children. Some didn't want to dredge up past deep emotions or risk being wounded by expressing this hurt. No one wanted to hurt those they loved, and I had to respect that not everyone was equally ready or willing to expose these raw edges of their family's lives.

But because these stories were so helpful, I felt compelled to pursue them. I knew this process had to start with me; I needed to share our family's story, even though I didn't want to betray my own children's trust either. I understood a parent's reluctance to talk on record. I knew I too would have to make the difficult tradeoff between keeping confidences while sharing enough to be helpful. In the end, I chose to navigate this by sharing selective details and keeping every interviewee's identity in confidence.

Some people reading these stories may say, "What's the big deal? Why are parents whining about the equivalent of 'first world problems'?" They may believe that there are bigger problems out there to worry about. But at the same time, there are others who may wonder why parents are not *more* devastated at the faith transitions of their children.

The bottom line is all parents everywhere experience some degree of pain over their children's decisions, no matter how big or small. What seems crucial and dangerous to one set of parents may seem trivial and silly to others. The range of pain points in parenting is nearly as varied as the number of children we all have. For some parents, their pain comes from children going to jail or getting hooked on drugs, while other parents have sleepless nights worrying that their children *might* be headed to the wrong college, are getting bad grades, or aren't valiant enough in fulfilling Church callings. All stories of children straying from the expected path are unique, but what is not unique is the pain. It's safe to say that most parents experience disappointment with at least *some* of their children's choices, no matter the source. As author Elizabeth Stone once said, "Making the decision to have a child—it's momentous. It is to decide forever to have your heart go walking around outside your body."[1] Anytime we care passionately about something over which we have only limited control, there's bound to be some degree of pain involved.

This book has been written to help parents find peace in the midst of pain brought on by their children's surprising and jarring choices. I have chosen specifically to focus on the decision children make to leave behind active participation in the Church. However, there are many elements of the experiences shared here that may be generalized to people of other faiths, and to parents whose children are making other types of disappointing decisions. It's not unusual for children to walk away from their parents' dreams, and all parents everywhere need to figure out ways to deal with this.

This book is laid out as follows. The first chapter explores the experiences of some parents whose children have left Church activity. I have purposely chosen not to have the stories come from the leavers; instead, I focused more closely on the impact on the parents. The second and third chapters address the question of how commonly this experience occurs and why it might be happening. The fourth chapter examines why these departures are painful, and the fifth chapter explores some of the different ways parents react. Finally, the concluding chapters (six through nine) present an array of ideas on how people make their peace in the face of their children's faith transitions.

I was fortunate to be able to gather stories from a variety of sources. These included direct and group interviews with approximately twenty parents from across the United States. The parents I spoke with had experience in a range of Church leadership positions, including former Relief Society presidents, multiple former bishops, and members of stake presidencies. I was also able to speak with people whose family histories stretched back to the earliest pioneers, as well as more recent converts. I interviewed families who had both daughters and sons leave the Church. All of the people I spoke with had leavers in their twenties or teens. Throughout the book, all names (and some details) are changed to respect people's privacy.

Chapter 1

How Does It Feel When Children Leave?

What happens to parents when children decide to step off the gospel path? How do parents feel? What makes these feelings worse or better? Of course, parents react differently, depending on personal circumstances. While some may not be as concerned, others are utterly devastated. This chapter is an attempt to understand some of the range of parents' responses to having children depart from the Church.

The first step many parents take after a child's departure is to try to figure out what happened and why. They look for the logic behind their child's actions. In some cases, parents can see the writing on the wall and have anticipated their child's departure for years because of past actions or experiences.

But in other cases, children seem to take this step away because of puzzling bouts of apathy toward beliefs and practices that matter most in their parents' lives. Or kids may step off the path with surprising quickness by following a friend, falling in love, making a mistake, or in any number of other ways. No matter what the child's motivation, parents often feel guilt and embarrassment, and too often their reactions only serve to make matters worse. These feelings seem to be compounded when parents have multiple children who choose to depart.

Tanya

Tanya was a parent to departing teens who was willing to share her story with me. When Tanya's daughter Erica started to drift away from the Church, Tanya could not understand why this was happening. She couldn't point to anything in this daughter's life that would explain why she would so easily abandon her parents' cherished beliefs. When Erica left home for college and quit attending church altogether, Tanya was baffled by her daughter's apathy. She described her daughter's attitude by saying, "She seems completely indifferent to the Church. She'll come if she's home, but she has a sour expression the whole time. And we have to wake her up to get there." Tanya could not pinpoint any compelling reasons for her daughter to leave, and she remembered when her daughter's testimony had been solidly age-appropriate during her teen years.

The only thing Tanya could think of was that a boyfriend had entered the picture during high school. He had sometimes made disparaging comments about the Church and was perhaps too intimate with her daughter. Tanya guessed that these things had eroded her daughter's faith. Tanya also recalled that Erica had many friends who were living lifestyles contrary to gospel teachings, and this caused her to question her beliefs.

The result was that when Erica went off to college, she just "acted like it was too hard to get to church." It was apparently too far to walk, and she did not make the effort to find rides. So Tanya and her husband decided to eliminate that excuse by buying Erica a car. They didn't really *want* her to have a car, and she didn't need one for any other reason, but they felt this was a cause worth supporting, even though it would be a substantial financial burden for them.

Erica, in the meantime, was not doing well on other fronts. She had health issues and was becoming depressed. One day, when the brand-new car was already sitting in the driveway, ready to hand over, Erica told her mother, "I don't believe in the Church. I never have. I hate being Mormon. I don't know if I believe in God."

Tanya was completely taken aback. Why was her daughter feeling so negative about the Church? Where were these feelings coming from? There were other clues that Erica needed medical care, so Tanya brought her daughter home from college for treatment. She discovered that Erica's physical health issues were affecting not just her mental health but also her spiritual health.

After this traumatic experience, Tanya and her husband mustered all their powers of persuasion and talked their daughter into going to BYU. She attended as a transfer student and seemed to like BYU for a short time. But then her depression caught up with her again, and she was hospitalized. Fortunately, her stay was short, but since that time, Erica hasn't shown any enthusiasm for church.

When I talked to Tanya, the pain from her child's decisions reflected in her entire being. She told me that when she first learned of Erica's decisions and experiences, "I felt like I couldn't breathe. I felt like I died, but I knew I was still alive. I wanted to go back in time before these things happened, so I would wake up and they would not be true." While she realized that she honestly did not have control over Erica's decisions, she still felt terrible about herself because of her child's decisions and actions. In Tanya's words, "I used to feel like one of the winners in life, but now I feel like a loser." Some mornings, Tanya would wake up and feel utter discouragement because the pain was just so severe.

In the end, Tanya felt her fondest wishes in life might never come true: "I simply cannot have what I wanted." Her sense of powerlessness was perhaps the most difficult aspect. As she said, "I used to feel I had a measure of control over my life and what happened to me. I had confidence that if I had a problem, then I could fix it. I had all the will and I did everything possible, and it still didn't fix. It's so hard."

She saw her hands as being completely tied: "There are only a few things I *can* do and I can't do anymore. It feels like the more I do, the *worse* it is. It has to come from them. There's nothing I can do."

Beth

Beth is another mother who experienced the struggle of watching several of her beloved children drop their activity in the Church. For one of Beth's daughters, Christine, this did not come as a surprise. At age ten, Christine was asking questions like, "Why do men run everything—like the Church, the country? Why is God a man?"

Beth said she knew what was coming and thought, *Oh my gosh, I am in trouble.* She could tell Christine was not destined to be a typical Mormon girl. In junior high, she wanted colorful streaks in her hair. In high school, she wore surfer clothes and joined a punk band. When Beth called her children to gather downstairs for family home evening, Christine would ask, "Can we hurry?" Beth said to me, "I didn't have a lot of hope for her future in the Church." When Christine announced in her twenties that she was homosexual, Beth was not surprised. She had seen signs in her daughter's teen years and suspected this was the case.

However, the trajectory of Beth's son, Rob, seemed to give her more grief, perhaps because of the cumulative effect of having a second child depart from the faith, or perhaps because there were fewer early signs. When Rob was a teenager, his activity level in the Church was off and on. He experienced some wonderful confirming moments with the Spirit during youth activities such as youth conference and EFY, but then he would sometimes disappear during church and his parents would find him asleep in the car. He had a girlfriend during high school, and this led to more physical involvement than Beth thought appropriate.

During high school, Rob started walking home during church meetings. His popularity with girls only made it more difficult for him to live gospel standards. Beth and her husband decided to send Rob to a private school that they hoped would help instill better discipline and give him a change of scenery. This approach seemed to help somewhat, and Beth was delighted when Rob got into BYU. It looked like there was hope he might even choose to go on a mission. Rob made plans to room with a very rule-abiding friend, and prospects looked good.

But within a short time, Rob had to drop out of BYU because he wasn't living the rules. His girlfriend had an eating disorder and other mental health issues that also complicated both their lives. Rob joined the military and introduced a friend to the Church and even baptized him, but it soon became clear that he was not headed down the path to a mission. Instead, Rob was marching to his own beat and wandering away from Church standards.

Beth said that during this phase of her son's life, it became incredibly difficult for her to go to church. In their congregation, there were about twenty missionary-aged young men, so almost every other week, there was either a farewell or a homecoming for one of them. In Beth's words, "Some Sundays, my whole goal for the day was not to cry during church. It was really hard. I felt like I was wearing a hair shirt." She said that one Sunday, she burst into tears and could not stop crying. She had to leave the building.

It occurred to her: "I just can't go to church anymore because this is so painful." She felt like she had failed because her family wasn't all active, and she wondered how this could have happened. She said, "I felt like I had spent all that time in the Church on my callings, driven all the kids to seminary, done all those things as well as I could, and then for it not to work? I wondered, *Why did I do this? Why isn't it working?* It feels like I am not part of this club. That was really painful too."

Samuel

Samuel was an active, involved LDS father and Church leader who had three children leave the gospel during their youth. Though one later returned, this exodus of his beloved children was heart-wrenching. He described the impact of this experience as being "like a rejection, not just of the Church, but also my lifestyle. . . . My kids could never fully realize why I was so dedicated to the Church. It was really difficult for me. I have no doubt I'm *not* a bad parent, but it still doesn't take away the loss I feel."

One of the biggest sources of pain for Samuel was his disappointment that he could not save his children from the consequences of their actions. As he said, "At the time, I was making the best decisions I could under the priorities I set, but perhaps I could've done better and spared them some pain. But you don't get two shots." He shared that it was even worse for his wife, who simply could not cope. "It tore her up."

Susan

Susan's experience with departing children may seem extreme. As her children reached their teens and twenties, each of her four children, one by one, decided to quit going to church. One daughter married a kind-hearted and religious young man of another faith, and is currently raising her children as active members of another church. She constantly does charitable acts of service for other people.

Several other children had difficult or embarrassing experiences during high school or college that coincided with their departures. All of Susan's children are doing good things with their lives, but none of them are currently attending the Church, and this has been painful for Susan and her husband. Susan is a strong member of the Church and a former Relief Society president. The Church is a huge part of her life.

During her children's exodus, she struggled with depression. To this day, she still feels moments of great sorrow. She said, "Sometimes I ask myself, 'How do you *do* this?' How do you get all your children to leave? After all those years of driving the kids to every single Church activity? Every day of seminary? Taking every calling? Going to every meeting? It seems almost impossible to me." And, in a lovely moment of humor, she said, "This feat should be written up in the *Ensign*!"

But the reality is, as she said, "I can't always laugh about it, obviously." Susan was grateful that after her children left home, she and her husband were assigned to another congregation where no one knew their family situation. Susan said it sometimes got so difficult that her husband advised her, "If you need to leave the meeting, just leave." She said to me, "The worst part is when I try to rewrite history. If I start thinking if only I had done this or that to help my kids stay in." But she added, "When you start reliving, you can get to a bad place."

One thing Susan found most difficult was hearing that she simply needed to try harder to get her children back to church. She recalled one incident when someone asked the teacher, "Do you think you need to keep trying *every day* to get your inactive children back?" The teacher answered, "Well, you better be!" Susan heard this as another reminder that she had failed as a parent and needed to continually try to rectify past errors, even though it was unclear what those errors were, or what could be done about them.

In reality, Susan realized on an intellectual level that this was not something she could fix. At a certain point in a child's life, parents simply can't be the ones to pull their children back. They must come back on their own. As Susan expressed, "I think one way to deal with this is you have to just let it go. The kids don't want to be hounded. And when you rewrite history, you take on blame that isn't yours." She also pointed out that it really wouldn't do any good to pester children on a daily basis because it drives a wedge into the relationship. She said, "I'm a firm believer that I am *not* a good nag."

The amount of pain these parents feel is sobering. It seems to be magnified when multiple children leave—and even worse if and when they leave simultaneously. It's also worse *while* it is happening. This may be because, during the departure period, it feels like any number of tiny course corrections could make the difference in the entire future of a child's life. Dieter F. Uchtdorf presented this concept in a compelling talk, in which he described a terrible plane crash caused by the pilot's miscalculation of only a few degrees. He pointed out that if you're traveling a long distance, such as around the entire globe, being off by only one degree in your flight plan can land you five hundred miles off-course. He stated, "All too often . . . we set out on what we hope will be an exciting journey only to realize too late that an error of a few degrees has set us on a course for spiritual disaster."[2]

When my second daughter chose another path, I was also frantic and distraught, like the parents described previously. I kept feeling that if I could just tweak the situation a little in the right direction, her whole trajectory could be easily and quickly set right again. I worried that if my daughter departed, it would just become harder and harder for her to return. My brain was spinning with thoughts like these:

- If her old friends would just attend with her and help ease the transition
- If she just took the right institute class
- If she had the right visiting or home teacher
- If I prayed hard enough
- If God came down with angels and struck her dumb, like Alma
- If her father, grandparents, or friends would just say the right thing

- If she happened on the right article or quote (which I may or may not have felt compelled to send her)
- If she would just pray
- If she would just read scriptures
- If she had the right experience that caused her to need the Church in her life

I wanted someone, somewhere, to do or say something that would work. But in the end, it was really about whether she *wanted* to go back. It was nothing I could control. This was a difficult time for me, and I spent many hours talking to anyone who would listen to me in my attempt to find the perspective I craved.

One snowy winter weekend during this time, a good friend was staying at my house to give a talk in our area. She thoughtfully listened to my woes and told me, "I have a talk for you to read." A few weeks later, she emailed me a talk by Virginia Pearce called "Prayer: A Small and Simple Thing," which was originally given at the BYU Women's Conference in 2011. I printed the talk but didn't read it for many weeks. I was skeptical that the talk would help, but even more worried that it wouldn't. Finally, one day, while engaging in my favorite coping mechanism of furious cleaning, I came across the talk in a pile of papers near my bed. I started thumbing through, and it opened to a story about a friend of the author she called Jane.

> Jane is a covenant-keeping member of The Church of Jesus Christ of Latter-day Saints. Her life has many facets: church service, full-time work, devotion to family, neighborliness, church callings. She is smart and funny and faithful. And, like all of us in mortality, she confronts heart-rending challenges—the greatest of which has to do with her family. As her children matured, some of them began to choose different paths. She witnessed them making choices that she knew would lead to unhappiness, and she was heartbroken—even frantic. She went over and over her parenting decisions of the past and was filled with guilt. Maybe this was all her fault. She found herself anxious and fearful—wondering what she could say and how and when she could say it so that the errant child would see the light and return. She worried about every interaction with the child—her own, as well as her husband's, the ward members', the neighbors'—everyone's! To say she felt tormented and out of control would be accurate.[3]

Chapter 2

Is This a Trend?

Since the beginning, parents have had to cope with their children's painful choices and shifts in belief. This phenomenon has been happening more or less continuously since Adam and Eve, but can we get a sense for how often children are departing from their religious traditions nowadays? There is some evidence that this experience is not as isolated as it may initially seem to those with a newly departed child.

One woman recently asked me, "Do you know *any* adult families who still have all their siblings and parents active in the Church?" This is a question worth pondering. While many young families with little children are all active, it seems that by the time people reach the gray-haired years, it becomes much less common for an entire family to stick to the faith. While it appears that there certainly are such families, some would claim that if you look deep, nearly every family has at least someone somewhere on the family tree with a difference of belief or faith. Not surprisingly, the parents of youth who are departing report that this state of affairs is quite common. According to one father, "Virtually every family faces one or more major moral crises." One interviewee speculated, "I don't think there's a family in my congregation that hasn't been through *something* with their teenage kids. As soon as parents have teenagers, I never assume they don't have problems." About half the time, she said, she finds she's right.

Are an increasing number of LDS and other religious parents seeing their children take other paths? What do these numbers look like? This can be a difficult question to answer because Church-wide statistics are not available, but there is evidence that this is a problem for more than just a tiny minority.

Not surprisingly, numbers from one East Coast stake show that Church activity rates drop off as young people get older and choose for themselves whether they want to continue to remain religiously engaged. Looking at activity levels from 2011 to 2013 in this stake, a high percentage of Primary children are active (89 percent). The number of teens between ages twelve and seventeen attending church remains relatively high for girls (77 percent) and boys (61 percent). But by the time young people hit the emerging adult ages from eighteen to twenty-five, the number of those still engaged in the gospel shows a big drop down to just over one-third still active (36 percent).[6]

Activity trends in other Christian churches follow a similar downward trajectory. In the book *You Lost Me*, author David Kinnaman reported that many youth (43 percent) drop out of church between teen and early adult years, thus becoming "the black hole of church attendance."[7] For all Christians, well over half drop out at some point after going regularly in their youth, and about a third of all Christians go through a period of either significantly doubting their faith or wanting to reject their parents' faith.[8]

There is clear evidence that religious involvement has shifted dramatically in just a few years among all Christian religions in America. The 2014 Pew Study of Religion and Public Life reported that between 2007 and 2014, the percentage of people in the United States identifying themselves as Christian dropped from 78.4 percent to 70.6 percent—a nearly 8 percent decline![9] Many of these people then claimed to be atheist, agnostic, or "nothing in particular." In contrast, among Church members, these numbers have remained virtually identical over the same time period, with the number of Mormons dropping from 1.7 to 1.6 percent of the population. This is a much better statistic, but it also suggests that, at least recently, the Church is losing members at the same rate that missionaries bring them in.[10]

In a recent longitudinal study done in Southern California, sociologist Vern Bengston found that some religious groups fare better in passing along their religious beliefs to the next generation. In particular, Mormons and Jews tend to have a better track record than others.[11] Quentin L. Cook reassured members of the Church in April 2015, "The Church of Jesus Christ of Latter-day Saints has never been stronger," and that, over the last twenty-five years, the "number of members removing their names from the records of the Church has always been very small and is significantly less in recent years than in the past."[12] But Bengston found that even among the group of LDS families he examined in California, the percentage of families whose children carry on the family faith stands at 80 percent, leaving a full 20 percent who face this situation.[13]

In a talk given in 2011 at Utah State University, Church historian Marlin Jensen affirmed that, while the Church is vibrant and thriving, there have been some concerns that the rate of attrition from the Church has accelerated in the last five to ten years. In response, the Church has instituted a program called "The Rescue" to educate people about some of the confusing or sensitive topics from Church history and doctrine. Some of these topics have been addressed in the "Gospel Topics" section of lds.org.[14]

LDS Church leaders are not the only ones concerned with and working on this issue. Many people in and out of the Church have noticed this trend and are working to understand it better and try to help those who are considering departing. Outside the LDS Church, there are programs like "StickyFaith" designed to "build lasting faith in kids."[15] Inside the Church, some single adult conferences now tackle topics like, "Dealing with Doubts."[16] Several excellent talks and papers are available on this topic, such as Jay Richardson's "Carving a Place for Those Who Wrestle with Their Testimony,"[17] Terryl Givens's "Letter to a Doubter,"[18] and Jack Zenger's talk on dealing with doubters, given in a church meeting in Midway, Utah.[19] Former UCLA professor Bob Rees also has an excellent collection of essays from notable people in the Church entitled *Why I Stay*.[20]

Others have created podcasts and discussion groups for the purpose of helping people cope with doubts. Of course, efforts in this direction are not new, as there have been excellent articles in the past on similar topics, such as BYU professor Eugene England's article titled, "Why the Church Is as True as the Gospel."[21] The proliferation of new types of social media cuts both ways—people have greater access to troubling information but can also find faith-building resources more easily as well.

Why Don't We Talk about This?

If this is so common, why don't people talk about it more often? Why do people keep their familial struggles with inactivity so private? One of the promises members make when baptized is to help "bear one another's burdens" (Mosiah 18:8). But on this topic of children's choices to depart, parents are often reluctant to share. As one mother said, "We don't talk about these things. I don't even *know* whether people's children are still LDS or not." In some ways, this is a good thing. There is no need for a family members' Church activity to be the first thing out of a parent's mouth, but in other ways this comment reflects a stigma against revealing this particular type of struggle. Of course people don't love sharing that they don't have the perfect faithful family. But discussing these issues can be the first step to reaching a place of wholeness and healing. It can also help us understand this phenomenon better. In the next chapter, we look deeper into possible reasons why this trend is occurring both inside the Church and in other faiths.

Chapter 3

Seeds by the Wayside

One mother shared her teenage son's explanation for leaving the Church: "I just got tired of being the only one who couldn't do what everyone else was doing." Another father explained that when his daughter met her husband, "she loved him more than she loved the Church." But these simple comments do not tell the whole story. Most departure stories are much more multi-faceted.

One recent survey asked people to share some of the reasons why they left or stopped believing in the Church. The survey collectors received over three thousand responses from people who had been previously committed to the LDS faith but later chose to leave. The final list of reasons was thirteen single-spaced pages, and included scriptural, historical, social, cultural, and spiritual elements. Some people experienced family issues or had difficulties with leaders, fellow members, or friends. Some had qualms or disagreements about policies, practices, or historical conundrums in the Church. And sometimes people said it was because they basically no longer cared about their previous beliefs.[22]

Jesus Himself alluded to the notion that sometimes seeds of faith simply don't take. Instead of growing in fertile soil, these seeds sometimes fall by the wayside to be eaten by birds, on stony places with no soil, or among thorns that choke them. Without roots, they scorch in the sun. Jesus did not elaborate; instead, He left us to draw our own conclusions. He didn't even cast judgment on what happened to the seeds. He simply said, "Who hath ears to hear, let him hear" (Matthew 13:9).

On some level, we expect every departure story to be unique because all people's experiences and personality characteristics are theirs alone. A collection of these departure stories would make for a *long* list. But the broader cultural and historical context also plays a major role in these trends and help explain why departures may be accelerating. In this section, we look at some of these social, societal, and historical factors that appear to impact Church participation, especially among young people.

Religious Participation Trends

For some years now, people on the whole have become less and less likely to participate in churches, at least in America and Europe. People in these places simply are not as traditionally religious as they used to be. While researchers don't agree on the exact numbers, they do corroborate that "religiosity has declined with each successive generation."[23] For instance, the number of those who claim to have no religion has climbed drastically. In the twenty-five years since 1990, the number of adults in the United States who claim to be unaffiliated with any religion has climbed from 7 percent to nearly 23 percent![24] And for the younger crowd, ages eighteen to thirty, these numbers are even higher.[25]

Peoples' beliefs about God and where religion and spirituality should be practiced have also changed dramatically over the past generations since 1900. Since the early part of the twentieth century, people's beliefs in God have gone from an acknowledgement that God is all-powerful and observable through nature and everyday miracles to believing that God is "whatever you want it to be."[26] Similarly, people are now more inclined to believe that religion can be practiced "either inside or outside of Church."[27]

So what do young people typically say they *do* believe? Their beliefs reflect a great deal about what is currently going on in society. A research study of 2,500 young people by Smith & Snell revealed the following about what youth typically claim they believe.[28]

- God watches over the world and wants people to be good to each other.
- Sin and redemption aren't relevant.
- People don't really need God in their daily lives unless there's a problem.
- People won't go to hell.
- Nearly everyone will go to heaven when they die.
- God wants us to feel good about ourselves.
- People should be allowed to believe what they want.

Interestingly, people still seem to want to expose their children to religious education because they feel it will help their children grow up to be good people. Research attests that there are many benefits of religion. In both adolescence and emerging adulthood, "religious beliefs and participation are associated with lower rates of substance use, illegal activities, and sexual risk behavior (such as multiple partners)." Studies also show lower depression rates, better relationships with parents, and an increased likelihood of volunteer work in those who are more religious.[29] But in contrast to most LDS believers, and even though people seem interested in sharing faith with the next generation, most say they don't feel faith is necessary in their own lives on a daily basis.

Shifts in Family Norms

Changing social norms have also had a huge impact on church participation trends. Young adults in our era have grown up with drastically different social norms than their parents. Some of the greatest differences are in expectations surrounding families. People are marrying later and getting more education. One study showed a major drop in the likelihood that women will marry in their early twenties. In 1970, only 38 percent of women age twenty-four and younger were *not* married, but by 2005, that number had climbed to nearly 76 percent.[30] Undoubtedly, this number has climbed even higher in recent years. In 2012, a *New York Times* article pointed out the startling fact that "more than half of births to American women under 30 occur outside marriage."[31] What used to be called illegitimacy is now widely accepted as normal. In 1960, only 4 percent of single mothers had never been married; today, 44 percent of single mothers fall into this category.[32]

The entertainment industry regularly portrays lifestyles vastly different from the previous generation's weekly doses of *Leave It to Beaver* and *Little House on the Prairie*. To some extent, the practices encouraged by many churches don't reflect what young people are seeing in their current social context. In other words, many of the rules people learn at church are simply ignored by society, likely causing some unwelcome cognitive dissonance if and when young people attend church.

Women's Issues

Women's roles are also having a dramatic impact on this generation. Expectations for women have shifted greatly since the era of the Equal Rights Amendment in the 1970s and 80s, and such issues are coming to the fore for the Church once again. As society has grown to accept and expect greater equality between men and women, many committed LDS members are finding women's issues to be a sticking point.[33] Women have historically been the group most likely to accept LDS beliefs and stay active, but some of the Church's views and practices around women are causing consternation, especially for the younger generation.

Many asking these questions are faithful Saints who love the gospel and the Church. They are staunch advocates for their beliefs but are starting to wonder about women's roles in the Church. In an article on the Mormon apologetic website FAIR, author Neylan McBaine said that there is a "tremendous amount of pain among our women regarding how they can or cannot contribute to the governance of our ecclesiastical organization."[34] She also quoted one married female college professor who stated, "The only place in my life where I am treated like a lesser human being is at church."

McBaine described her experience as an undergraduate student in the Relief Society presidency at Yale University, when her greatest challenge was keeping other LDS freshmen young women active. "I struggled with finding ways to engage them, to make them feel needed, to give them jobs in our church organization that were more appealing to them at 9 a.m. on a Sunday morning than staying in bed and sleeping off that 3 a.m. dance party." But she bemoaned that there were no important tasks for most of them to perform at church, like those required of the young men: "After all, I couldn't ask them to get themselves out of bed to pass the sacrament." In her article, McBaine clarified that she was not asking for women to get the priesthood, but rather that she was hoping more will be asked of the women in the Church.

There is reason to believe this sticking point may be shifting because of the new missionary age for young women[35] and new opportunities for leadership for women in the mission field and other areas.

LGBT Issues

Another new reality of this generation is growing sympathy and concern about LGBT (Lesbian, Gay, Bisexual, Transgender) issues. One author suggested that this upcoming generation is much more concerned about LGBT issues because "their sense of community is more expansive."[36] Teenagers in many communities are exposed to anti-bullying campaigns in school, which have heightened their awareness of the issues of LGBT peers. The media also now portrays the LGBT community more positively than in the past.

Even the world of professional sports has started to be more open and accepting toward gays. In February 2013, Michael Sam came out as the first openly gay player in the NFL, followed by a survey from ESPN showing that 86 percent of the NFL claimed they would be okay with having a gay teammate.[37] With the recent 2015 Supreme Court ruling, gay marriage is now legal all across the country. According to a 2007 Pew survey, 60 percent of adults in the United States feel that homosexuality should be accepted by society.[38]

LGBT rights are a compelling issue for many young people, who take their attitudes of tolerance seriously. Fortunately, the Church is attempting to be responsive to LGBT issues in helpful ways, such as by creating the website mormonsandgays.com and by actively encouraging attitudes of tolerance and love for all. Yet it seems many LDS members see their own beliefs as being at odds with Church policies and practices. Their concerns over these issues threaten their belief in the Church and their willingness to participate. My conversations with parents corroborate that this is a relevant issue for their children who are leaving, and one that is not easily solved.

Technology's Impact on Religiosity

Another possible reason young people are leaving is also unique to our era: Who can tell how much technology has impacted this modern generation of "digital natives"? Young people who are constantly plugged into some type of media may simply find religious attendance unexciting and slow paced. It's not unusual to see teenagers and young adults down the aisles, texting or fiddling with their phones or iPads during church services. It's no wonder that this younger generation gets antsy during church and finds it difficult to sit through services. As psychologist and professor Jeffrey Arnett described, "The pace and peace of a typical religious service may feel to them like walking through the door to an earlier century, and it's a place where they may feel like strangers in a strange land. Everything about it . . . seems centuries old, a relic of an ancient (and much less entertaining) era."[39] Short of somehow adding additional razzle and dazzle to Church services, this is also a problem that does not lend itself to easy solutions.

Technology also affects people's willingness and ability to believe what they're told. This modern generation has greater access to information about Church history and doctrines, and there is strong evidence that this is causing a crisis of faith for some. One young LDS convert, who had benefitted greatly from his affiliation with the Church, was urged by a high school friend to look on the Internet about LDS history. He was surprised and embarrassed and felt betrayed by what he found. Within a matter of days, he decided to drop out of Church. Who knows what other reasons he had for departing, but this access brought him to a tipping point and over the edge. Jay Richardson described how those in the millennial generation seem to look at the world: "They have grown up in the information age. They have access to information at the press of a mouse button that in years past was the domain of scholars searching in dank old libraries. This infusion of information allows them to fact-check quickly statements made by authority figures. The Internet has also affected how they see the world, feeling more connected than previous generations to the global community."[40]

Technology certainly does have the capacity to bring about many faith-promoting resources into our individual lives, but at the same time it can be a double-edged sword by raising unhelpful questions and doubts in people's lives.

Emerging Adulthood Is a Time for Searching

As painful as it may be for us parents, if we had to pick a time when people *should* scrutinize their faith, it would be during young adulthood. This is a time when we honestly want our children to develop their own abiding faith, and that can only be done by placing that faith under the microscope. According to Jeffrey Arnett, young people in developed countries are *expected* to go through a period of soul-searching and reflection that helps them crystallize their beliefs and worldview. This phase is an earmark of growing up, tending to occur roughly between eighteen and twenty-six, in a phase he labeled "emerging adulthood."[41] Nearly a generation ago, BYU professor Stan Albrecht found this to be the age of greatest risk for people leaving their faith. According to Albrecht, if you have to pick the age during which people are most likely to disengage, it is during teens or early twenties, with the period of greatest risk between the ages of sixteen and twenty-five.[42]

One reason young adulthood is the logical time for religious exploration is because there are fewer constraints and expectations for this age group. During high school years, many parents feel the need to tweak, nudge, and even harangue their teens constantly to follow rules and get with the program. But when teens head off to college or out on their own, there is often much more freedom to explore and wander. This is the classic time for young people to push boundaries and rules. Even strict religious groups such as the Amish expect and allow a *rumspringa* period for their youth to run around and figure out what religious beliefs they will settle down with.

Of course, most Mormon parents are generally not in favor of the idea of a free-for-all period for their children, and they encourage kids to either completely skip this stage or shorten it as much as possible. Many urge their youth to go straight from high school to a church college or on a mission in order to minimize the chances that they will abandon the faith. When Church leaders recently shifted the age requirements for youth to go on missions at younger ages, this became an easier goal for parents to achieve. Now, many Mormon youth essentially head straight from their parents' homes into missionary responsibilities at eighteen or nineteen, jettisoning the exploration phase completely.

As a result, LDS youth miss some of the hazards of an exploratory period. While many young people are at the height of self-indulgent behavior, LDS youth are cementing ties to their beliefs as they teach Christian principles and observe the impact of those principles on converts' lives. So long as LDS youth actually do go on missions, they're much less likely to question the faith; instead, they become *part* of the faith as they work with leaders—and even *become* leaders in the Church. This allows them to see the great blessings that come into converts' lives when they embrace the gospel. In contrast, those who leave have a much harder time seeing the Church's goodness because they simply miss the view.

In essence, Latter-day Saint youth head straight into adulthood. They are encouraged to marry early and begin families at a younger age than most couples in the United States. As soon as these young people begin to have children and focus on raising the next generation, the luxury of exploring a "new" worldview is often subsumed in the feeling of responsibility for passing along positive values to their children.

Allowing Room to Doubt

Interestingly, there is some evidence to suggest that parents who provide children the freedom to question have better luck passing their faith along to their children. When parents overreact or dismiss questions, this strategy can backfire. Vern Bengston's research found that parents who push religion too hard or clamp down on doubt sometimes end up with children who rebel and defy their families' faith.[43] One interviewee explained that his divorced parents took different approaches to his search for belief in the Church. His father had completely abandoned belief, but his devout mother was nearly panicked that her son might lose his faith in God if he asked too many questions. As a result, this man said he felt freer to examine his faith in God while at his father's house because he knew his father would not implode if he made "the wrong choice" about what to believe. In the end, his testimony was strengthened at his father's house.

This chapter has provided a brief look at some of the reasons this current departure trend is happening and seems to be accelerating. In the next chapter, we look at some of the reasons why these departures can be so difficult and painful for parents and other family members.

Chapter 4

Where Is the Pain Coming From?

Most parents understand all too well that both joy *and* pain are part of the parenting package. Of course, they anticipate the joy, but sometimes the level of pain catches them off-guard. And the particular pain of a child choosing a path away from the faith can be particularly wrenching. A few years ago, a large group of LDS parents were given a choice of talks to attend at a conference held at BYU. One talk titled "As Parents, What Do We Do with the Pain?" was originally scheduled for the super-sized ballroom that seats over a thousand people, but because attendees were so drawn to this topic, it had to be moved to the huge campus arena that accommodates over 22,000 people.[44] Clearly, many LDS parents don't get off scot-free from the emotional toll of childrearing!

There are many reasons parents feel fear and pain for children, but there are some unique features of the pain caused by children who depart from a parent's religious tradition. As Bengston described it, "To religious parents, faith forms the core of what is most valuable to them in life, what has meant the most to them, and what they would like their children to live by."[45] When children reject their parents' faith, it can be incredibly challenging. Arnett acknowledged that, for some parents, "their grown kids' religious choices are an emotional flashpoint." He continued, "When parents' religious beliefs are central to their worldview and daily lives, what their children come to believe . . . may be one of the most important measures of their success or failure as parents."[46]

Mormons Are Not Alone

It may help to realize that this parental discomfort over children's religious choices is not exclusive to Mormons. People in many religions hope their children will cling to their beliefs and suffer when they don't. One work colleague shared that whenever he visited his parents, his father would invariably bring up his beloved Catholic faith and hound his fifty-year-old son to come back to church. My colleague felt skewered and uncomfortable, and his solution was to simply quit dropping by to see his parents as often. His mother finally caught on to this and warned her husband that unless he could leave the subject of religion alone, they would not be seeing their son all that much.

A formerly Jewish mother found that when she chose not to circumcise her infant son, all of a sudden family members bombarded her, trying to get her to change her mind. They sent her articles about every possible health benefit of circumcision. They wanted to hold onto the hope that the baby would one day be able to go to Hebrew school, have a bar mitzvah, and possibly marry a nice Jewish girl. But to their dismay, this young mother was willing to close that door forever and said no.

Another acquaintance shared that the only reason he no longer felt guilty about leaving the church of his childhood was because his parents were deceased. "But," he said, "if they were alive, I'd be hearing about it from my mom."

Mormons may not be alone in how they experience the effects of a child's departure from religion, but there are some reasons why LDS parents may feel these effects more acutely.

Mormons Have High Expectations for Family Togetherness

First of all, Mormons have high expectations that everyone will stay in the faith. Even though people in other churches push their children to stick with their faith, LDS families may be unusual in the degree to which they encourage every single member of the family to continue participating, with no exceptions. One woman I interviewed shared how difficult it was for her to hear a fellow ward member publicly celebrate their last child going through the temple, with all of their other children and spouses able to join them. She said, “It’s so hard when I think that’s not going to happen for us, when really that’s all I’ve ever wanted. I don’t care about other things nearly as much. Of course, I would like them all to graduate from college and have good careers, but honestly, that’s way down the list from all of us being united in how we feel about the Church.”

Another woman expressed her discomfort during a talk she heard about a family with multiple generations still active—over a hundred of them without even a single young man missing his responsibility to go serve a mission or a single young woman missing her opportunity to marry in the temple. Some Church leaders have become attuned to the awkwardness of moments like this. On one occasion, the visiting authority got up after one of these public celebrations of family solidarity and requested that speakers consider their audience and try not to burden the rest of the congregation with their successes.

Some of those I interviewed came from families whose ancestors and current extended family members are all in the Church. They expressed gratitude to be part of this collective culture of cohesion. At the same time, they recognized that they felt a great deal of pressure to keep up the family record. As one mother expressed,

> I often heard my grandma speaking with great pride how everybody—fifty-six cousins in all—were still active. In that entire set of cousins, there was not even *one* single male who had *not* gone on a mission. One wall in my grandmother’s house is filled with photos of the missionaries who have gone, and the other wall is filled with photos of the temple weddings that have happened. That’s a big deal for my grandparents, and they talk about it a lot. And it’s part of our family culture. Our family is on this path, and we’re are all moving together—and there’s no gray area. A lot of our family has felt that it’s good pressure, but I don’t know. It’s clearly pressure for me. I have lost sleep worrying about my children making other types of choices.

When the entire rest of the family is in, losing a first family member can understandably provoke anxiety. One mother shared her memory of her brother breaking the family record for her parents by being the first to leave the Church.

> Of the thirty grandkids on my dad's side, my brother was the only one who didn't go on a mission. He was the only atheist and the only one who didn't marry in the temple. I was much younger and the only one home at the time this was happening, and I remember how this impacted my parents. Then he married a Jewish woman, so it became even clearer that this was the path he was staying on, and I saw the intense pain my parents felt—and I felt that vicariously too. They felt they were the ones who failed. What's that quote about no other success compensating? My dad wasn't out there having any grand career or making lots of money. He lived a life of Church service, but he just beat himself up over his son's choices.

In this woman's case, she felt kind of relieved when other family members stopped the winning streak by not doing everything perfectly. She said that when she heard about a family member getting divorced, "I was sad for her, but another part of me was saying, 'Phew, the spell is broken.' In my generation, it was my brother, and now it's their family line that messed up the record."

It's extremely helpful to be aware of the existence and power of these strong norms to stay in. Some of my interviewees felt there was a lot to be said for this kind of pressure. But some people on the outside looking in see that Mormons push themselves hard. One of my religiously unaffiliated friends once gently chided me, "I've noticed that you Mormons are always comparing yourselves to each other, and your children to your friends' children. You're so hard on yourselves!" The pressure to keep every single family member in the faith can make those whose children are outliers feel even worse. This does not mean we necessarily want to alter this culture, but it does help to understand ourselves and know where this pressure is coming from.

Mormons Have High Expectations for Their Children

Another contributing factor is that LDS parents' expectations for their children's behavior are high, making it that much easier for children to fall short. One woman I interviewed pointed out, "We have so many expectations on us. . . . We have such a narrow range of permissible behaviors. I have noticed that some parents in other churches don't really seem to mind what their kids do. Their kids can go nuts, get drunk every night in college, and wake up not sure where they are, and their parents *expect* that. It's so much easier for our children to go off the deep end." For Latter-day Saints, the "deep end" covers a large territory. While this mother had no wish for the Church to lower its standards, she was acutely aware of the challenge this presents for youth and the parents attempting to instill these standards in children.

In a recent article in the *New York Times* by Yale wife and husband team Amy Chua and Jed Rubenfeld, the authors held up the Church as an example of a religious group able to coach their people to succeed to an unusual extent.[47] How do Mormons pull this off? They do this by teaching children they are exceptional, by holding them to some high standards, and expecting a great deal of impulse control. And it's true that LDS parents ask a great deal of their youth. Consider the following: when LDS children are little, they learn to sit through three hours of Church, something many adults find challenging. When children are a bit older, they're encouraged to fast, abstaining from food and water for at least two meals. Youth are taught not to swear or be unkind. They're asked to give up fun activities with friends on Sundays, like birthday parties and sports. As kids hit their teen years, they're coached to wait until sixteen to date, to avoid drinking alcohol, to serve others and set goals, and—at the age when youthful bodies crave sleep most—to attend early morning religion classes every day before school. And of course, chastity is a given. While most young adults are exploring freedom and diving into self-absorption with gusto, LDS youth are encouraged at age eighteen or nineteen to sacrifice a substantial amount of time to serve missions. After all of that, they're expected to obtain higher education and marry at a relatively young age. Talk about impulse control! LDS parents start when children are young and don't stop until kids are married and trying to instill the same values in the next generation.

Because LDS families push kids to do more and be better, they definitely can achieve a great deal, but there are also risks. Not everyone can or wants to keep up this rigorous pace. While we all desperately want to succeed with our families, it's apparent there are simply so many different ways to fail. At any point along the journey, kids can make a misstep, and off the path they go. One LDS young man who was struggling with his life challenges told his parents, "I used to know what my path would be. I was going to graduate from high school, go to college, go on a mission, and then get married. Now I'm not so sure where I'm headed." It was a poignant and painful moment for that family as he considered dropping out of high school and the Church. Another mother shared that her daughter did everything as expected for many years, starting with reading the entire Book of Mormon before age eight. But as she got older, this daughter didn't follow the expected family timeline to get married before graduating from college. Her mother worried and said, "Our culture is so strong, and I can sense it becoming harder and harder for her to keep coming and feeling a part of things."

While we don't want to change these high standards, it's useful to keep an accurate perspective on just how rigorous these standards are in today's world. There are many, many ways for kids to fall off the path and flounder for a time.

Parents' Feelings of Personal Failure, Guilt, and Blame

When children don't adhere to every expectation, parents often blame themselves for their children's decisions. They feel they have failed on some level, and the guilt can be intense. It can be particularly jarring when parents compare themselves to other parents who appear to be doing everything right. One man shared, "I think my pain was increased by the idea that lots of other families were succeeding and that ours wasn't. I wanted to hide our private realities."

It was common for those I interviewed to do a quick mental calculation about the percentage of kids in versus out. And in general, parents with multiple children out tended to feel worse. One father said, "Well, I'm at 25 percent of my children active, and that is not too good." Another mom whose children were all out, was completely baffled by her track record, wondering how it was even possible to have all her children leave the Church after trying so hard to keep them all in.

One former Church leader recognized that even though he wasn't a bad parent, he still felt a terrible loss when his daughter rejected the Church. He said, "It's always a question of whether you should have done something different. But you can't redo. When you're looking for fault, the first person to blame is yourself. I felt that in one part of the exercise, I did not do too well." He went on to clarify that even though he never felt like he lost his daughter completely, he wished he could have done better and "spared her some pain."

Another father I interviewed expressed his pain over his teenage son who was swayed by what he read on the Internet and no longer believed in the teachings of the Church. This father said, "I feel like I've failed him. That's the honest-to-goodness truth. I think that if somehow I had done better, he would be on a different trajectory in terms of his faith." On one level, this father knows his son's beliefs aren't his fault but stated that it's still difficult to see his son departing before he has enough maturity to see for himself just how "deeply good the Church is." As this father said, "I went on a mission. I worked hard. I was so obedient. I studied so hard. I was really good at the language, yet I didn't baptize a single person on my mission. You would think I would have learned my lesson about the power of people to make their own choices, but clearly I haven't learned that well enough." And he is still feeling that responsibility acutely.

Another father, who was a bishop several times over, felt a great deal of personal responsibility for his sons' decisions to leave. He said, "My most prevalent thought was that if I had a stronger testimony, this wouldn't have happened." Though this man was a much-loved bishop, he said, "I still don't see myself as an exemplary Latter-day Saint." He wished he had done a better job communicating his spiritual experiences to his sons. "If I could raise my boys now, and tell them what I know now, it might be different."

Hopes for Family Cohesion

Parents also dread having family members head off in different belief directions because they want cohesion in their family. They want to be able to speak the same language and appreciate the same things in the same ways. One person lamented that having her brother outside the Church had changed the dynamics in her family.

It bothered her that sometimes her brother and his academic colleagues would "make fun of the Church." She said, "He tries to be respectful around me, but he's crossed the line before and hurt my feelings. It changes things."

Another mother shared that conversations are definitely different now that two of her children have quit going to church. When her children were little, she said, "We could all be talking about gospel principles and how we felt about life, and then we were all on the same page. Now, we are all conscious of how our words are affecting those who disagree. Some get a little edgy, and this dynamic is not what I want."

One woman said it took her some time to figure out what she could still talk about to the kids. "You just can't say anything. You can't talk about the Church around them, at least not in a pointed way—like, have you talked to so and so yet about that? But you can tell them what you're doing in the Church." Other parents found that they had to simply stick to safe topics, like sports, children, cooking, or work.

Conversations between parents and the grandparents can also get a little touchy after children leave the Church. Parents must navigate difficult discussions about the status of their children in the Church with grandparents, who also have a stake in their grandchildren's faith. One mother reported how difficult it was for her when her mother would start off each phone conversation by asking, "Has our granddaughter gone back to church yet?" She wanted to reply, "Trust me, if she returns, you'll be the first to know."

After some of these tough conversations, some parents are left feeling like they no longer want to communicate with extended family members as often. Some even choose to quit sharing accurate details of their children's lifestyles. One grandfather asked his son about his granddaughter, "So, Bridget is completely active in Church and has tattoos?" The father's response was, "Yup, that's right," simply to avoid the conversation altogether. Others choose to omit specific details of their children's lives because, as one person put it, "that's not a burden grandparents should have to bear."

Other parents have coached their families to quit asking *only* about the child who is having issues with their church-related behavior, rather to start by quizzing them about other family members first. And some parents simply pull back and communicate less, as did this woman, who said, "It's made it so I don't call home as often. They'll ask about things, and I just don't want to tell them. I don't want to articulate it. I also don't want to break down, and I know I am more likely to when I'm talking to them. If I talk to them, I just feel so, so sad. I'm less likely to call them, and that makes me even more sad."

These pointed conversations can also be difficult for the children flexing their wings. These *rumspringa* youth are often dismayed by all the extra negative attention they receive because of their behavior. One disaffiliated son told his mother he hated the thought that the ward leadership discussed him in ward council. He did *not* want to be the ward's project. Another wandering daughter made her mother promise not to talk about the Church when she was around, unless the conversation wasn't directly pointed at her. She put her siblings and parents on notice by saying, "If I come to church, I don't want anyone smiling and looking happy about my being there, at least not in front of me."

Worry for the Child

Likely the biggest source of anguish is over the child's current and eventual spiritual well being. Parents worry what will happen with a child's eternal salvation. What about the family being together forever? And in the meantime, what will happen to the child making harmful choices that compromise their health and happiness? What parent wants to watch his or her child in misery? One father spoke of the pain he could see in his daughter's eyes in her online photos, following her departure from the Church. The daughter he had helped raise to be sweet, radiant, and joyous was now weighed down in trouble and conflicts with others. He said, "She is now sometimes very, very sad, and that is difficult to see. I wish she could see what is causing her this anguish."

Even for those children who seem happy out of the Church, parents worry they won't experience the opportunities to serve others and give back to their community. One father shared his sadness that his non-participating sons were missing out on important personal development. He said, "I tell them people have a spiritual life too.

Not everything is intellectual and physical." He added, "I tell my son, 'You have that too, but you just don't acknowledge it.'" Another mother expressed her dismay that her daughter wasn't able to serve in her community because, without participation in the Church, there were no built-in mechanisms to foster those opportunities.

This chapter has examined some of the reasons parents don't sleep well at night because of concerns for their children's spiritual safety and growth. It's difficult for parents when they feel they are the only ones who cannot manage to keep their children involved in the Church. These parents hate breaking family traditions. They feel bad when children have to experience the pain of their own destructive choices, or simply cannot find as much happiness as they otherwise would. Parents mourn for the elusive cohesion that other families seem to have and they feel responsible for their children's choices. All of this puts parents in a difficult spot, and they sometimes feel isolated and alone. There are few supports available through official Church channels. But there is hope. In the next section, we examine some of the possible reactions parents can have when children journey outside the fold.

Chapter 5

Parents' Reactions

When a child makes the choice to leave the Church or the LDS lifestyle, parents have to decide how they will respond. One LDS father was asked, "Would you still love your children if they told you they were gay?" His answer was, "No, I would not!" One mother was unhappy with the wives her LDS sons had chosen to marry. She expressed, "My children know that my love is *not* unconditional."

Another set of LDS parents broke ties with their returned missionary son after he moved in with his girlfriend. They insisted he bring back the car they had given him and take a bus back home. When the son later married his girlfriend, his parents emailed one word: "Congratulations." They didn't attend the wedding, and they weren't invited. To this day, two years later, the parents are barely speaking to their son and new daughter-in-law.

Columnist Robert Kirby recently wrote a column in the *Salt Lake Tribune* about parents who reject their children for not believing in their faith and concludes that sometimes religion can be a tool for "silently torturing loving relationships to death."[48]

Of course, parents cope with the disappointments of their children's choices in ways that make the most sense to them at the time. For some, it may seem that their only option is to reject their child, which makes it possible to compartmentalize the pain and keep it manageable. It's tough to feel accepting and loving toward people whose actions you don't approve of. But there is a clear downside to this choice—the loss of very important relationships. Elder John K. Carmack cautioned parents in this situation that "harsh and judgmental reactions," or "threats to disown" children, do not help. "Because our children follow a different course than we have taught them does not give us license to reject them."[49]

One mother chose a different kind of reaction following her son's departure from the Church, which she shared with me in an email, which read as follows:

> A few years ago, I was feeling like such a failure as a parent as I watched our son Gabe not just quietly slip into inactivity but vocally and deliberately make it known to us that he no longer wanted to be part of the Church, and that it was his choice to leave. And that is what he has done—he's left the Church. I thought back to all the things we had done wrong, the times where we didn't read family scriptures, the FHE nights that were lame and had no spiritual element to them, the ways in which I had failed to teach him how to feel the spirit. My list of failures is endless.
>
> Fortunately, a few things happened over the course of a few years to help me get things in better perspective. One was the tender mercy of being in a class about the Fall and the Atonement. As we reviewed the plan of salvation, I realized that our heavenly parents *knew* my pain—they too had lost a third of their children in [premortality]. These spirit children had said, "No, we don't want to follow what we have been taught; we choose to follow Satan's plan." I'm sure our heavenly parents suffered greatly when this happened—suffered like I was suffering. That understanding made me realize that perhaps Gabe's choices where not all due to my failure, but rather, like all God's children, he was exercising his agency, as is his right and gift to do.
>
> After talking over my heartbreak with my wise uncle, he said something to me that also gave me perspective. He reminded me that our children have a lifetime to sort out their lives and their choices. He said that life is long—in fact, it is eternally long. Hopefully our kids will sort out their testimonies sooner rather than later and come back to the gospel in this mortal part of life. Very likely they will. But

if it doesn't happen then, it will be in the part after life where they gain their understanding, make their amends, and come back.

My uncle also reminded me that our children are sealed to us for the eternities. If my husband and I keep our covenants, those promises will be honored. Gabe is sealed to us here and will be in the eternities, one way or another. He may require some additional teaching and some additional repenting on the other side of the veil, but if we stay true to our covenants, he stays sealed to us. On occasion, I have reminded him of this. I've seen a glimmer of a smile on his face when I've said that we are a family forever, and that he is coming with us. We love him and we are not leaving him behind. I think that brings him some comfort, even though he would never admit it at this point.

Finally, I had a chance to teach a lesson on the Atonement. And, as always, I feel like I learned so much more than those I tried to teach. I had an insight into how the Atonement can work in my daily life. I realized that growing up with inactive parents, I had never had a strong example of how to teach my children to feel the Spirit, to gain a testimony, to be strong in the gospel. My parents had never taught me these things. To make things harder, I married a convert, who also had no example to follow in terms of raising children with strong testimonies. In many ways, we were the blind leading the blind, and that was no fault of our own—it was the circumstances in which we were raised. We did the best we could, given what we knew. And we fell far short, despite doing our best. I realized in preparing this class that I could turn to my Savior and say to Him, "I did the best I knew how, and it wasn't enough. Can you help me make up the difference? Can you atone for where we fell short?" The answer is, of course, a resounding yes! Somehow, somewhere along the way, Christ will make up the difference of what we didn't or couldn't do for Gabe.

I have a quote framed on our wall that Elder Quentin Cook quoted in general conference a year ago. The saying is, "To believe in God is to know that all the rules will be fair and there will be wonderful surprises." Whatever the wiring or the shortcomings that my husband and I had as parents or whatever the "unfairness" is for us regarding Gabe, in the eternities it will be made fair and there will be wonderful surprises. I believe Gabe will be with us.

Gabe's mother found an oasis of peace in an otherwise bleak desert of disappointment. She was able to stay connected to her son, and she still has a great deal of hope.

There are many other parents who share her perspective and have acted accordingly. In my numerous interviews with families, many have found ideas and strategies that have helped them make the best of a heart-wrenching experience. They have managed to keep strong, positive relationships with their loved ones, even though they no longer share the same bedrock beliefs. They have chosen to think and act in ways that help them bridge the gap between themselves and their children.

Even though there are many different approaches parents can take when children leave the gospel, there are some essential elements common to all who successfully maintain close relationships with their children and find some degree of peace.

First, the parents who find peace *accept* their children as they are, *take some action* to reach that reconciliation, and hold on to *hope* that things will work out for the best. These are the core ideas of the next few chapters. Parents who find peace learn to balance these complex emotions of acceptance and hope and find the uneasy truce between them.

For many, accepting children as they are requires a substantial shift in thinking about the way parents believe things *must* and *should* be. This can take some time. Parents who maintain relationships with their inactive children also need to take important action steps. They really have no direct control over what their adult and teen children are thinking, so all efforts to change must be pointed toward themselves.

Finally—this step gets to the crux of the paradox—while parents accept the current reality, they can still hold onto the hope that things will change for the better someday. I present these concepts as separate and concrete, but in reality all these techniques and perspectives are inevitably intertwined.

Undoubtedly not every perspective will seem equally helpful to every person. What works for your in-laws or best friend may not be what is most helpful to you. The goal here has been to provide a range of ideas that have worked for someone, somewhere, and at some point in time in the hope that some of this collective wisdom will help readers find the solace, perspective, and peace they seek.

Chapter 6

What Works: Accepting the New Reality

When a child departs from the faith, it may seem impossible to accept that this is the new reality for the family. But as one former bishop put it, "Beginning with reality is a much better way to deal with issues than beginning with the way things *should* be and trying to force them into that mold." Especially right after a child leaves, it can be extremely difficult to accept this new reality. One parent whose children abandoned faith shared, "The beginning is the worst, and time heals. I had to get accustomed to the idea." Parents can't expect to adjust immediately. They need time to go through the stages of grief. It's a process. The pain may not go away, but it does become less jarring over time.

One mom found that when she was saying, "But I *need* my children to be doing this or that" or "I *wanted* this experience for them," she was miserable, and so were they.

As long as she was saying things *should* be a certain way, she wasn't able to feel love, acceptance, and the spirit of God, and this made it impossible for her to experience gratitude for her children. And she said, "They *get* that. They know I'm not feeling grateful for them." She found she had to get to a place where she could accept the reality she was currently facing, even though it was certainly not her first choice for her kids.

Love What Is

When my own much-loved daughter was starting to turn away from the Church, I was not by any stretch of the imagination ready to accept this new reality. I didn't appreciate that she was flexing her wings or testing her faith. I just wanted her back. I could barely think or talk about anything else to anyone. I was a walking mess of emotion and misery, and nearly every quiet moment was filled with anxiety and hand-wringing over my daughter's actions. She was two thousand miles away, but she was always on my mind. When I would get into a car and think about her, tears would start pouring out of my eyes, and I couldn't seem to get the perspective and peace I so wanted and needed.

About this time, we were eating dinner with friends, and before long my daughter's story was spilling out of my mouth—again. We loved and admired these friends and respected their wisdom. This couple had also experienced several children departing from the Church. The husband was serving as the bishop of a neighboring ward at the time. He asked me some important questions from a book by Byron Katie called *Loving What Is.*[50] I found these questions to be completely eye-opening. He asked:

1. How are your thoughts making you feel?

2. Are you absolutely, positively sure your thoughts are true?

3. Can you think of one stress-free reason for holding onto those thoughts?

4. How would it make you feel if you did not believe those thoughts anymore?

These questions stopped me in my tracks. I knew I was jumping to some long-term conclusions about my daughter that I couldn't necessarily assume were true. I was taking for granted that her non-participation right now meant all kinds of extra things, such as:

- She will never return to the Church.
- We will never be a close family again.
- She will not be a nice person.
- People will think less of our family, and me.

- I will be sad for the rest of my life.
- This is a tragedy.

Perhaps such thoughts resonate with other people? When spelled out like that, some of them may sound immutably true while others sound completely unsupportable or even irrelevant.

When I actually considered what it was I was thinking would happen because of my daughter's actions, I realized that it was actually my *assumptions* and *thoughts* that were making me miserable. In the end, I realized that I couldn't prove any of these ideas were necessarily correct, and I had control over my reactions and thoughts, starting with my assumptions, each of which are worth looking at more closely.

Assumption 1: My daughter will never return to church

I realized that I certainly couldn't guarantee that my daughter would never return to the Church. In fact, as I started to study and learn, I found that there are still a lot of reasons to hope for her future reconciliation with the gospel.

Assumption 2: We will never be a close family again

I realized that I still have a great deal of control over whether our family remains close, and that there are many steps I can take to help us remain connected to each other. I recognized that I needed to reach out to all my children more often, encourage them all to reach out to each other, and figure out ways to keep close ties and enjoy each other's company, in spite of our differences of opinion and lifestyle.

Assumption 3: She will not be a nice person

I fully recognized that my daughter was still a nice person. In fact, she seemed to actually start compensating for disappointing me in the Church realm by reaching out to me more, so long as I was willing to leave the topic of religion aside and talk to her about other things. I started noticing and appreciating all the ways that she was still the child I had raised to be conscientious and appreciative. I was more attuned to her goodness.

Assumption 4: People will think less of our family

This was an assumption that I couldn't completely evaluate because I couldn't get into the minds of our friends and acquaintances. But I reminded myself of the families that we revere in the scriptures who had experienced the pain of children's choices. Were people judgmental about those exemplary families? I felt I was in good company there, and I needed to not worry about this possibility, primarily because it was out of my control.

Assumption 5: I will be sad for the rest of my life

I soon realized that being sad for the rest of my life just wasn't an option for me. I didn't want to be sad forever, and I knew I had a lot of control over my emotions. Time heals, and I recognized that there were things I could do to help me feel better. I realized that my daughter's actions did *not* have to determine my mood forever. Fortunately, my life is full of many good things, and holding onto sadness didn't make a lot of sense.

Assumption 6: This is a tragedy

I quickly recognized that this was a tragedy if I considered it to be one, but there was nothing cast in stone forcing me to consider it that way. Perhaps this phase was actually an important step on her life journey. In fact, I recognized that it wasn't my place to judge whether this was a tragic step for her, but rather to leave that in God's hands.

One mother enlightened me on this topic. When her son was of missionary age, she went through a long process of realization that he wasn't going to serve a mission. This was devastating to her for many reasons, but eventually she decided to simply stop pulling so much meaning from her thoughts at every moment. As she said, "The thought that Todd had to go on a mission for me to be happy wasn't working for me so I let go of it. When you need other people to be a certain way and do certain things, that is a *surefire* recipe for unhappiness, and 100 percent guaranteed to fail. Why would I want to set up my life like that?"

It can be immensely helpful for parents to recognize these discouraging thoughts for exactly what they are: thoughts! They aren't yet reality, and it's perfectly reasonable to argue with them. While it's natural to worry, it isn't always useful and can often get in the way of finding peace and helping others. As Todd's mother explained, "What's most important is learning not to worry, because when you worry, you can't give peace and happiness to others around you. Our minds will always look for danger and things to worry about. They were designed that way. But we can learn that just because we think a thought, it doesn't mean it's true." Likewise, those thoughts don't need to make us feel miserable.

Todd's mom also explained that sometimes those with children who have left the gospel fall into another thought trap she called "reverse pride." This happens when people compare their challenges to others' and imagine that their lives are much harder. As she said, "You can get a little affirmation out of that. Part of you is rewarded by thinking negatively." But if you continue on that path of negative thinking about your family situation, it will just land you in a puddle of self-misery. And our lives here are about finding joy, which is certainly possible regardless of our children's choices.

Children's Choices Aren't about You

It can be freeing to realize that our adult children's choices are theirs, and theirs alone. When my children were little, I did everything in my power to help them make good choices. I tried to teach them to love the gospel, choose good friends, use their time well, be kind to others, and work hard in school and life. I threw myself into parenting with all the energy I could muster. I really enjoyed being with them! We baked together, worked together, held Family Home Evening, read scriptures, talked long hours, took field trips, and created fun memories. We were incredibly active in Church, virtually never missing a meeting. I thought I had the whole parenting thing down, and I thought they were a lovely reflection of my parenting prowess.

But when they became teenagers, it wasn't so easy to nudge them in directions I liked. They exerted their will. They didn't always want to follow the rules. They didn't all want to do their homework. They weren't always easy to get along with. Some didn't want to go to church. They all did different things for different reasons. They were complicated! I can safely say none of my four children were easy, but all of them were hard for different reasons. There was no one-size-fits-all formula that worked to keep them in line. Sometimes I just wanted a guarantee that I was doing things right, and they were going to turn out okay—or better yet, the way I wanted them to be. But that just didn't seem to be the way things were headed.

During one particularly challenging time when our son was struggling terribly with schoolwork and other life challenges, I had an epiphany. It may sound less than spectacular now, but it was quite a revelation to me then. My children's behaviors were not about me. I had taught them. I was doing everything I could think of to set a good example and teach them correct principles. As they became young adults, it became time for them to govern themselves. I would have taken away their agency and made every decision for them if I could, but that obviously wasn't really an option. Now it was their turn to make their own decisions, and their choices didn't necessarily need to be a reflection on me. They weren't *trying* to wound me, and I could choose whether to be wounded or not. In the end, they were going to live their lives, and I could either kick against the pricks and fight that or accept that they were going to make their own choices. Of course, I would continue nudging as much as possible, when possible, but it didn't make sense to feel too much personal responsibility when it wasn't mine to feel.

Some parents seem to have a gift for keeping their children's actions separate from their own identities. They don't see their children's behaviors as reflections of themselves. This makes it much easier for them to find peace with their kids' actions. One father shared that others' opinions of his wandering son simply didn't matter to him. He had found that Zen zone where he could just not worry about what other people thought.

In his case, he learned from the example of a family relative what *not* to do. This man's aunt had four sons who had all left the Church. Prior to their leaving, though, she was always delighted to announce to others when her sons became leaders in their missions, or when they were called as members of bishoprics. This woman built her pride and identity around her children's Church roles, but later found that identity to be a house of cards. When her four sons left the Church, her self-image crumbled. As her nephew explained, "There's definitely a certain pain when kids make choices we don't like, but it multiplies exponentially when you build your world around those children's choices." As Elder Carmack said, "Parents and children will get along much better if parents avoid living through the achievements of their children."[51]

One mother found it extremely important to keep a centered perspective after her third child began choosing a non-Church lifestyle. She said, "I think I was finally able to realize this is not about me. This is her life. I don't own her. Eventually, people become what they're going to, and my child is not a checkmark. My daughter's decisions about the Church aren't who she is. I cannot reduce her to her choices." And this mother still adored her daughter because, as she said, "Plus, she's just so dang lovable."

This mother found it freeing to realize that she was not responsible for what her child thought, and she was able to look past this daughter's decisions to the core person inside. She knew she had an obligation to teach her children important principles, but it was their stewardship to determine what they did with that knowledge.

Let Go of Blame and Guilt

One important goal is to let go of blame and guilt. Many parents I interviewed mused that things might have turned out better if they had just been better parents. But they also acknowledged that this thinking led nowhere good fast. One mother said, "One way to deal with this is that you just have to let it go. When you rewrite history, you take on blame that's not yours." In this woman's case, her non-attending children insisted that she is *not* at fault: "My kids are always telling me that it wasn't me. I'm not the reason they left." They constantly remind her: "Mom, we have a good family. We're all good friends. That's what we wanted."

Over time, this woman has come to appreciate the blessing of her close family—with all their wonderful conversations and get-togethers—and turn her focus away from feeling guilt for their departures from the gospel path.

Parents' Righteousness Doesn't Absolutely Determine Their Children's Choices

One helpful perspective to remember is that parental righteousness has never correlated perfectly with children's choices and is definitely not the only determinant of those choices. Parents do make a difference, but there are many other factors at play. Some children have an inner spark within that drives them toward religion and belief, no matter what their parents do. They may be the only active member remaining in their family, or the only convert. One woman shared with me that when she was young, none of her family members were attending church, and life was tumultuous at home. Yet she felt the pull of the gospel and walked by herself to church. She simply wanted to be there. A teenager I know feels the pull of Church so strongly that she prods her four younger siblings out of bed on Sundays, finds them rides to and from church, and makes sure they all get there. To this day, she urges them to go because she knows it will be good for their futures, and she loves the gospel. She does this in spite of the fact that her mother never attends church and her father abandoned the family long ago.

These are remarkable people, and who are we to say why this happens for some kids and not ours? Obviously, not everyone feels the call to religious participation equally; it can be reassuring to remember that activity in the Church can never be 100 percent attributed to parental influence.

Sometimes it seems that some children are bent on heading away from the gospel. They're going to leave no matter how many commandments the family follows during their youth. One speaker at the BYU Women's Conference shared with her audience that her family had read the Book of Mormon together more than forty times! To let the full weight of this achievement sink in, she brought a wagon to the podium heaped with over forty copies of the Book of Mormon, representing each time her family had traversed its pages. Still, she admitted that her family had their struggles, and at least one of their children had chosen a different path.

This shows that great valiance on the part of the parents doesn't always translate to great valiance on the part of the children. One of my interviewees found this comforting. She said, "I blame myself and feel I did some things wrong. But I also feel some parents do everything right and things still go wrong."

It's not accidental that two of the most prominent families in the scriptures—Adam and Eve from the Bible and Lehi and Sariah from the Book of Mormon—had wayward children, yet we honor and revere them. There are plenty of other examples of righteous parents in the scriptures whose children didn't follow their ways, including Samuel, Saul, Abraham, and Alma. We can be grateful that we aren't given an example of perfect families to live up to; instead, we have families in the scripture stories we can *relate* to. When we read the scriptures, we can look at them and say, "Well, at least our children don't want to kill each other."

One mom found the examples of struggling parents in the scriptures personally reassuring. She stated, "Thank goodness we don't have an example in the scriptures of a family where every single member of the family for many generations never had a question about his or her testimony! Heavenly Father must have known we would get discouraged too easily if that were the case." Speaking of Adam and Eve and Lehi and Sarah, this mother said, "Both these sets of parents did their best to keep their covenants, but they were still human and led imperfect lives. They had imperfect and sometimes angry children, and they also had some amazing kids who followed their CTR rings to a T." Her philosophy was, "Sometimes Heavenly Father sends rebellious children to strong parents. I think Heavenly Father likes to mix it up and see how we do." And, as she pointed out, "Families that don't have a wayward or rebellious child really miss out on some growth." But she added that they may have other challenges that also teach them similar life lessons in other ways.

One interesting question to ponder is whether only the best and easiest children go to the most faithful and deserving parents. If we believe our children's righteousness isn't necessarily a reflection of our own worthiness, it makes their decisions much easier to bear. One Church leader I interviewed raised this exact question: "Sometimes you wonder if living a righteous life means you get righteous kids. Or maybe there are other reasons for getting challenging kids. Maybe you can turn them around? Maybe you can do as well as anyone else? Maybe you can do better? I don't know about the theory that since you're an A student, you get all the best kids. I think God just wants us to do our best for our children overall. It helps me to consider that kids don't come to earth with clean slates. They arrive here, and lots of things have already happened."

One LDS family therapist, Carlfred Broderick, agreed that we don't really know why some parents are blessed with tougher or easier kids, but he suggested that some parents might have actually chosen tougher assignments.[52] While Broderick was a stake president, he worked with a family whose children were venturing into inactivity. According to him, the mother "had made some very poor life choices," including marrying a handsome young man with terrible habits like gambling, drinking, and other spiritually damaging practices. Her husband joined the Church to marry her in the temple, but he quickly returned to his former lifestyle. "But the greater pain came when her children, having these two parental role models in front of them, began to follow him. He would say things like, 'Well, you can go to church with your mother and sit through three hours of you know what, or you can come to the racetrack with me, and we'll have good stuff to eat and drink and have a great time." It was a tough choice for the kids, and often they would go with their dad. They gradually seemed to adopt his lifestyle, values, and attitude toward the Church and sacred things. Though their mother never wavered from her own faithfulness and commitment to Heavenly Father, her family was slipping away from her.

President Broderick was called in to give this struggling mother a blessing to sustain her through her difficulties. He said that he felt somewhat judgmental, thinking. *Didn't you ask for this? You married a guy who really didn't have any depth to him and raised your kids too permissively. You should have fought harder to keep them in the Church rather than letting them run off to the racetracks.* But in the moment when he laid his hands on her head, he felt strongly of the Lord's love for this woman. He said he realized that his own children would have been good if they had been orphans, but he felt that this woman had made a choice before she came to earth to take on more difficult children. "She had signed up . . . for children who had rebellious spirits, but who were valuable; for a hard husband who had a rebellious spirit, but who was valuable." As he described it: "I repented. I realized I was in the presence of one of the Lord's great noble spirits, who had chosen not a safe place behind the lines pushing out the ordnance to the people in the front lines as I was doing, but somebody who chose to live out in the trenches where the Lord's work was being done, where there was risk, where you could be hurt, where you could lose, where you could be destroyed by your love. That's the way she had chosen to labor."[53]

Of course, we all want to do our best with our own children. We want to strive with all our might to help them gain testimonies. But in the end, we must realize that some of their decisions are out of our control. Many factors impact them, and we only get to affect a subset of what will ultimately keep them in or out. Even if we don't get a say in selecting our children's personalities in advance, we do know that it's up to us to do our best with the challenges we're given. After all, we are in good company with some of the most prominent scriptural families in the Church, and with Heavenly Father himself, who also lost many of His own spirit children. Perhaps we chose this adversity in advance, or perhaps not. Regardless, we can be grateful for the challenge and skip the self-blame for children turning out as they have.

Instead, we can look at challenges from children differently—as opportunities to grow instead of evidence that we have failed. Brigham Young stated: "If members of the Church had the eternities in full vision before their minds, there is not a trial which the Saints are called to pass through that they would not realize and acknowledge to be their greatest blessing."[54] If we wallow in guilt and blame, we're missing the point. Instead, we need to appreciate our children for what they have to teach us and continually strive to be the best parents we can be, no matter what curve balls are thrown our way.

Embrace Your Children's Agency

LDS doctrine teaches that agency is integral to God's plan for us. We got to choose before we came to earth whether we would follow Satan's plan to force us to obey or God's plan to make our own decisions. Most parents are only partly kidding when they say they like the idea of Satan's plan. It sounds so nice in theory to be able to guarantee that children will do what you want. But of course, this isn't possible, or even really appealing in the long run. Our agency is a great gift, and ideally we will embrace our children's agency as much as we value our own.

One mother exemplified this appreciation for agency. Her daughter was making choices she did not like—including living with different young men, using drugs, and posting inappropriate photos online. Nevertheless, this mother said, "Every time I get upset about how she's acting, I come back to appreciating agency. We fought for agency. That's why we got to come here. I'll rejoice in her agency. As a parent, I liked Satan's plan, but seriously, you have to like your children's agency." We all have to appreciate the gift that our children make their own choices because that is God's plan. Unless our children have agency, they will never gain a full-fledged testimony of their own.

See the Value in Doubts and Questions

It's helpful to remember that we actually *want* our children to discover their own testimonies. As was explored earlier in chapter four, we expect young people to go through a phase of asking big questions, determining their own worldview and finally what they believe. During this phase when young adults are examining belief, there is always the risk that they will turn away and choose another path. Some families deal with this conundrum by assuming there will be no questions at all.

One of the parents I interviewed had come from a long line of devout LDS family members. She couldn't recall anyone in her large family who had left the fold and become less active. She felt that much of this could be attributed to the fact that their family runs on certainty, not doubt. She said, "In my family, it's the certainty that has led hundreds of people to remain steadfast, where the link has not been broken. No one talks about any uncertainty." But at the end of the day, she was left to question whether this strategy actually worked: "There seems to be a formula in my family that works, if this is what you can define as *working*. But I am not sure how everyone really feels."

For many families, however, someone does open Pandora's box of questions. People question and doubt, and doubts carry the risk that some may decide to leave. But there is potentially great value in doubting because, without the existence of doubt, certainty is not possible. Philosopher Rene Descartes once said, "If you would be a real seeker after truth, it is necessary that at least once in your life you doubt, as far as possible, all things." One of my favorite lines from the book *Life of Pi* affirms this too: "Doubt is useful, it keeps faith a living thing. After all, you cannot know the strength of your faith until it is tested."[55]

Noted LDS thinker and bishop Terryl Givens clarified the benefits of a thorough examination of one's belief systems. He wrote that doubts aren't something to fear, but rather something to embrace:

> Be grateful for your doubts. . . . I know I am grateful for a propensity to doubt because it gives me the capacity to freely believe. . . . The call to faith is a summons to engage the heart, to attune it to resonate in sympathy with principles and values and ideals that we devoutly hope are true *and which we have reasonable but not certain grounds for believing to be true.* There must be grounds for doubt as well as belief in order to render the choice more truly a choice, and therefore the more deliberate and laden with personal vulnerability and investment. An overwhelming preponderance of evidence on either side would make our choice as meaningless as would a loaded gun pointed at our heads. . . . What we choose to embrace, to be responsive to, is the purest reflection of who we are and what we love.[56]

There is a cost to squelching all doubts in our children and loved ones. Sometimes our efforts to steer belief in certain directions can backfire. Christian minister Sean McDowell shared his firsthand experience with young people losing their faith and gave this advice: "Don't fear doubt—I have the privilege of spending time with many atheists and agnostics. When I ask them to share their stories they often say something like, 'I grew up in the church but it never made sense to me. My questions were suppressed and considered sinful. Eventually I just couldn't believe anymore.' "[57] McDowell pointed out that because of the Internet, "young people have access to every conceivable worldview." For this generation, "doubts are natural for this generation, and we ought to invite tough questions from young people. The key is not to give pat answers, but to teach them *how* to think."[58] His suggestion was that we do our homework, work through our own doubts first, and ask them good questions in response to theirs.

Parents will do well to remember that unless children are allowed the freedom to question and wonder, their testimonies will remain potentially fragile and immature. Some may only consider these questions fleetingly, or they may enter a prolonged period of examination depending on their predispositions. But these doubts can actually be seen as a great gift, so long as in the end the issues worth doubting can be separated from those that are rock solid. As one father I interviewed expressed, "Certainty is the enemy of faith. Questions and doubts are the ally of faith. If you can allow for the question, but hold onto what you believe, instead of this search undermining your faith and causing you to wonder about whether this is all built on a house of sand, it makes you realistic about things. Of course, there are things I have great certainty about, and my doubts cannot touch those." That's the kind of testimony that's durable and resilient. When tough questions arise, this kind of testimony has staying power.

We All Have Different Gifts

Another helpful perspective is to recognize that, in the final analysis, each of us is given a different capacity to believe and accept what we're taught on faith. There is no such thing as a level playing field when it comes to belief. Our children come to us with many aspects pre-wired—including possibly their capacity to embrace the gospel. One interviewee mused, "Do some families get the obedience gene?" Another friend stated bluntly, "I think the ability to believe is genetic." In her case, several of her siblings were finding it challenging to accept what they had been taught, and she felt it was simply more difficult for her family to feel the Spirit and exercise the gift of faith than others she knew.

Some people seem blessed with the ability to sense and appreciate the spiritual realm to a remarkable degree. Others have abilities that are more logical and observation-based while finding concepts in the spiritual realm elusive. They don't feel the Spirit the same way as others, and in some sense can't. They are just less sensitive spiritually, and it does not appear to always be caused by disobedience to commandments. People within the throes of depression, for example, seem to find it more challenging to feel the Spirit of God and to recognize His hand in their lives. In some cases, the same is true for some whose talents lie along the autism spectrum. Perhaps our brains don't all have the same capacity to listen to the Spirit and comprehend the messages being sent. And certainly these capacities can be impaired by experiences.

In other words, if we assume some receive great spiritual gifts, we must also assume others may have spiritual disadvantages or challenges. Interestingly, the scriptures support this concept. Doctrine and Covenants 46:11–14 tells us that we are given different gifts in our ability to believe:

> For all have not every gift given unto them; for there are many gifts, and to every man is given a gift by the Spirit of God. To some is given one, and to some is given another, that all may be profited thereby. To some it is given by the Holy Ghost to know that Jesus Christ is the Son of God, and that he was crucified for the sins of the world. To others it is given to believe on their words, that they also might have eternal life if they continue faithful.

In other words, some are able to have a direct knowledge of Jesus Christ, while others have the capacity for a more tangential knowledge, based on others' beliefs. This lends support to the idea that we are all able to feel the Spirit and accept the gospel in different ways and at different levels. This does not excuse us from teaching our children to the best of our abilities, but it does help us to recognize that there are many factors involved in our children's decisions to stick with the Church.

Savor All the Other Positive Qualities of Your Children

When my children were in preschool, I remember asking my visiting teacher about her teenagers. Without skipping a beat, the first thing out of her mouth was, "Well, Matthew is inactive," followed by some details about how he had left the Church. When I got to know her better, I asked her to tell me more about Matthew because I was confident he had many other wonderful characteristics besides this one choice. As she talked more about him, I was fascinated to learn that her son was a brilliant computer scientist, precociously well paid at a young age. He was saving the world from nasty computer hackers! But my friend's pain at his choice to leave was ever-present and overshadowed her ability to enjoy her son's other remarkable qualities.

Since then, I have been struck by how often I have had this same experience with members of the Church I barely know. Sometimes the only factor people mention about their children is whether they are in or out of the Church, as if nothing else matters. Our children's Church status does not need to be the first and only descriptor we share about them or define them by. Even people who make harmful choices have valuable qualities.

Many parents have found ways to appreciate and value their children without focusing exclusively on their departure decision. One father said, "It may sound obvious, but we just treat our kids like people. We don't tiptoe around Church subjects, and they are very supportive of us." Even though this man's son went through a period when he said derogatory things about the Church to bait his parents, he has since apologized for that phase and now quizzes his father about his experiences in the temple and as a bishop. On the day his father was sustained as bishop, this son was there. This father and mother said they have come to a point where they recognize there's no use being devastated about their children's Church status because that isn't going to help. They try to keep the most positive perspective they can.

Other parents focus on the various ways that their children who are outside the Church are doing good out in the world. One mother was asked in Sunday School whether she continued to pray for her inactive children. She used this opportunity to express appreciation for her daughter, who had recently called for a family fast to help cope with a family crisis. Even though she was no longer LDS, this daughter was still a spiritual person, living a generous and conscientious lifestyle and using helpful spiritual tools she learned in her upbringing.

Another LDS mother acknowledged that her inactive daughter might actually be happier at the moment than she was because, as she said, "She is working in a caring profession, and actually she is doing some things much better than I do. The career she chose helps people every day."

Another interviewee pointed out that even though his brother is inactive, he still loves his children and is a really good father. He said, "Our Church doesn't have a monopoly on goodness."

One mother expressed admiration for a family in her ward who succeed at affirming all of their children equally. She said, "They talk about their inactive children the way that they talk about their active children. They're proud of all their children, and see their good qualities. I just feel like they've figured out how to love life even though their children have made these choices, and it doesn't seem to be killing them. If my children left, I would want to be like that." When families are able to express this attitude of acceptance, it gives other families in their circles an example to live by. One father of a gay daughter who had left the Church said that it helped him immensely to know other people in his ward who were loving and accepting of their own inactive children. He realized that if he had to choose between having an active child who was unpleasant and nasty or an inactive child he really loved and enjoyed, the choice would be easy: he would pick the child he could enjoy. He felt grateful to be able to relish his relationship with his daughter, even though she doesn't fit the typical LDS mold.

Some congregations exemplify this type of love and acceptance in spite of young people's unconventional choices. One mother shared that when her son returned home from his mission six months early because of depression, her ward was incredibly supportive and understanding. The stake presidency thanked him for his service and acknowledged that his medical condition made a mission more challenging for him. No one looked askance, and this young man was able to make the transition to a full and active life within the Church.

Another mom shared that when her gay son showed up at church with his wild hair and earring, her ward members were always thrilled to see him. She was so appreciative that they just wrapped their arms around him and loved him the way he was.

In the end, we all benefit if we can see the good in our children and steer clear of judgment. Elder Dieter F. Uchtdorf made this point beautifully in his talk during the April 2012 general conference:

> I don't know exactly how to articulate this point of *not judging others* with sufficient eloquence, passion, and persuasion to make it stick. I can quote scripture, I can try to expound doctrine, and I will even quote a bumper sticker I recently saw. It was attached to the back of a car whose driver appeared to be a little rough around the edges, but the words on the sticker taught an insightful lesson. It read, "Don't judge me because I sin differently than you."[59]

Of course we all sin differently! It's so reassuring to know that Heavenly Father accepts us *where we are*, no matter whether our mistakes are big or small. In fact, Heavenly Father's goal may simply be to take us from where we are and nudge us a little farther down good paths. That is a worthy goal for parents too. How much easier would it be for all of us if we focused more on nudging and less on judging? We give our children (and ourselves) a gift when we see our children's inherent goodness, in spite of the choices we don't love.

How many parents have children who turn out exactly as planned? One woman stated unequivocally, "None of our children turn out to be exactly the people we want them to be, in every single way."

Parents can hope and pray and assume children will do what they expect, but in the end children make their own choices, which sometimes lead them in healthy and positive directions and other times not. It's up to parents to love and enjoy their children in spite of whatever choices they make about activity in the gospel. Elder John K. Carmack put it this way:

> We can and should expect much of our children, but we cannot force them into the Lord's mold. Our children will not stay with the Church and live the gospel unless they *want* to. Once their wayward children grow up, the time may come when the parents will need to adjust their present expectations and approach, accepting things as they are rather than continuing in turmoil. We should not expect perfection in our children but, rather, adopt in patience and love the Lord's eternal view of things.[60]

And as one mother aptly put it, when dealing with children who have left the Church and the gospel path, "it's all about acceptance, acceptance, acceptance."

Chapter 7

What Works: Take Action

PSYCHOLOGISTS TELL US that one of the best ways for people to think new thoughts is to do new things. So how can we circumvent misery and think in new ways about our children's goodness and contributions? What can we actually do to reach a point of greater acceptance of our children? This chapter offers useful action steps for getting from pain to peace. This list includes forgiveness, prayer, getting educated, reaching out, giving love and service, and sharing our stories with others. While there's nothing novel about these strategies, they can make a huge difference in helping parents mentally get from Point A to Point B in terms of accepting their children.

Turn the Other Cheek

Parents may not always recognize that this is necessary, but the first action step may very well be forgiveness. Parents suffer when kids leave, because a rejection of parental beliefs hits at the core of what seems most valuable to parents. They may not even realize that they're angry at their children for causing them pain, but it makes sense that they would be, given the high stakes involved.

Psychologist Jeffrey Arnett said that he was sympathetic to such situations, but he urged parents not to criticize and reject "young people for their beliefs (or absence of beliefs)" because it "will not bring them back to your religion."[61] Instead, Arnett encouraged any parents struggling in these situations to forgive: "'Turn the other cheek' may be the wisest course for parents here. The best way to persuade children of the value of your faith is to show the fruits of it in your life, including your capacity to forgive your sons and daughters for not believing what you believe."[62]

Prayer Can Help Give Us This Perspective

A second action step is remarkably simple. We can pray. Prayer is accessible to everyone; all it takes is time and mental focus. Prayer can be the deal breaker in being able to accept and love our children and gain a measure of peace instead of being tied up in a knot of self-pity and misery. When one couple realized that two of their teenagers were headed away from the Church, the first commitment they made was to pray vocally on their knees each night, both individually and as a couple. After keeping this commitment for some weeks, the mother described the following experience:

> During this time, I was really, really having a hard time, and my husband was always having to "talk me off the ledge." During one of those times when I was just overwhelmed and pleading with God to somehow help me, in the middle of the prayer, what came to me was, "Ask a different question." I realized I had to just stop being so frantic, and the question I needed to ask was, "Are they loved?"
>
> So I asked the question, and it was life-changing. I was so overwhelmed with how loved and aware of my children God is, and how precious they are. Every time I struggle, I come back to that. I know every time I worry and how much I mourn for the disconnection and their turning away and how much I would do anything, that's nothing compared to what God would do for them. It bowls me over how clear it is that our children are precious."

Each of us is also entitled to the peace that can come from heartfelt prayer. In my own prayers for my children, I have been grateful for promptings to say or try something new with them to help them with their faith. On one occasion when my son was struggling with church attendance, I felt prompted after praying to just let him wear whatever he wanted to church. So for a few weeks, he passed the sacrament in a plaid shirt. While it was uncomfortable for me to see him break white shirt norms, it seemed infinitely better for him to be there in plaid than absent. On other occasions, my prayers have helped me feel better about my children's choices when there was really nothing I could do to change them. It has also been helpful to me to have paper and pencil nearby during prayer so that when answers came, I could record them. Our prayers may not bring our children back, but they can help us reconcile ourselves to where they currently are.

Temple Worship

Many parents find that attending the temple is another source of peace and hope during difficult times with children. Temple attendance can help us solve even our thorniest challenges. As John A. Widtsoe wrote, "I believe that the busy person . . . can solve his problems better and more quickly in the house of the Lord than anywhere else. . . . At the most unexpected moments, in or out of the temple will come . . . as a revelation, the solution [to] the problems that vex his life."[63]

One mother felt prompted to commit to weekly temple attendance when her children started pulling away from the Church. She felt her temple attendance helped her stay spiritually centered, and she invariably gained new insight while there. During one of the sessions, she felt blessed to understand that she needed to "lay on the altar" her expectation that her circumstances *needed* to be a certain way. She said it became apparent that as long as she was feeling that "things *should* be a certain way," she could not feel love and acceptance for her children or the Spirit. Going to the temple regularly reignited her gratitude for her kids and assuaged her daily feelings of discouragement.

Get Educated

Parents have access to excellent resources that can help them better understand children who have left. Elder John K. Carmack suggested that parents of troubled children seek help from medical science, especially for children with drug and alcohol issues.[64] There are excellent talks and podcasts available for parents whose children have doubts or lifestyle issues, and there are also helpful Church resources and websites that can give parents perspective and insight. Knowledge is power, and the more parents understand about what children are experiencing, the more they will know how to remain connected and helpful.

Talk to Departing Family Members in Helpful Ways

In a recent Relief Society lesson, the teacher shared with the class her heartbreak over learning that her brother had left the Church during graduate school. She wasn't sure what his issues were because she had not yet had the nerve to talk to him about it. But she was spending many hours worrying, to the point that it was causing her to have nightmares about her own children one day leaving the Church.

It's not easy to talk to family members in the process of leaving. People may share some of the following worries: perhaps the disaffected person will say something disturbing about cherished beliefs? Perhaps the person still in the Church will say the wrong thing that will drive someone further out? If the person with intact faith hopes to say the right thing to bring the disaffected back, that puts even more pressure on the situation.

Some of the best advice I have heard is to simply set aside a time to sit with the questioning family member and listen to his or her concerns. It may be helpful to set ground rules so that the tone of the conversation stays respectful. But there is no substitute for communication to achieve understanding.

Institute teacher Jay Richardson offered pointers for keeping these conversations productive. First, he cautioned members not to assume that young people with questions are simply covering up their sins with questions. He said, "First and foremost, please be careful not to reduce this complex phenomenon to simply a matter of sin." Second, he urged, "Please resist attempts to find a root cause that involves not praying or reading scriptures enough. Please do not let this be the first thing out of your mouth when someone opens up to you about their struggles. Often you will do more damage than any good that can come from trying to find some root cause of their immediate concerns."[65]

Another caution from Richardson was that we stay away from "either/or" thinking when discussing the truth of the gospel with those who are questioning. We shoot ourselves in the foot when we propose "either the Church is from God and thus true in all its teachings, or it is the worst fraud perpetuated on humanity, born in the pit of hell with Satan as its author."

Richardson said further, "If we boil things down to an either/or proposition, we are setting ourselves up for potentially damaging consequences." He found that many of the people leaving were stuck in this mode of bifurcated thinking. They ran across one "chink in the armor, one anomaly, one objectionable teaching, policy or practice and toss every religious belief away, no matter how powerful the spiritual experiences were that produced belief."[66] Instead, he suggested that we allow ourselves a little more leeway in how we think about the history and doctrine of the Church.

It can be helpful to acknowledge in these conversations that even though Church leaders are trying their best to do the will of Heavenly Father, they are still human and imperfect, just as we all are. As Elder Faust explained, sometimes members act like Church leaders are infallible, even though they "make no claim of infallibility or perfection in the prophets, seers, and revelators."[67] Of course there are some sticky issues in our history and doctrine if people dig deep enough, because we are part of a human-led, albeit divine, organization. The question is whether there are enough reasons to still remain—which there definitely are!

Reach Out to Stay Connected with Children

Sometimes it may seem easier to let our communication with our wayward children wane. After all, here's this source of pain, reminding us of our presumed failings. And often the children themselves are not doing much to stay in touch. How much effort are we really supposed to put forth? My own feeling is that staying connected is a worthwhile and important goal whenever possible. One interviewee told of some family friends who made ongoing communication with their struggling child a high priority: "Our friends are going to be mission presidents, and are some of the most wonderful people ever. Their daughter was a drug addict and stole from them for drug money.

They have been through everything with their daughter, but they have the best attitude. They just give her as much love as they can. They call and leave loving messages. They do whatever they can think of and hope someday she will come out of it."

Just when our children are doing their best to pull away may be the time when they most need us to reach out after them and show gratitude for their finer qualities. As one mother expressed, "I try to take every opportunity to let the kids know I love them, that I am grateful for every moment." Other families have figured out lists of safe topics to address with their children, like sports, grandchildren, and upcoming plans to get together. All of these can make a huge difference in finding eventual acceptance and love. Of course, sometimes children simply refuse to let parents stay close. As a social worker once explained to me about my own strong-willed daughter, "She won't *let* you be the kind of mother you want to be." But it never hurts to keep on trying to reach out.

Accept Your Parenting Successes

Every Church member grows up hearing the familiar quote spoken by David O. MacKay: "No other success can compensate for failure in the home."[68] This comment has spurred many people, especially fathers, to spend more time at home focusing on parenting. But, as Elder Carmack pointed out, sometimes parents misapply this quote and feel like failures, no matter how hard they have tried and no matter what other successes they may have achieved in their lives.[69]

In these cases, it's helpful to recognize that this quote does not mean we should define parenting success along only one dimension. Even when children leave the Church, we do not know whether they have left for good. Being raised in LDS homes likely helped them become better people than they would have been otherwise. In the original source for President McKay's quote, written in 1924, author and sociologist J. E. McCulloch gave a broad list of goals for parents to teach children: "The home is the first and most effective place for children to learn the lessons of life: truth, honor, virtue, self-control; the value of education, honest work, and the purpose and privilege of life. Nothing can take the place of home in rearing and teaching children, and no other success can compensate for failure in the home"[70]

Raising children is a multi-dimensional undertaking, and we need to focus on the many ways we have succeeded as parents in other areas besides participation in the Church.

Fortunately for us, in this arena of life, parents get to be graded on effort as well as results. The Lord knows our hearts and minds and gives us credit for our hard work, even when we cannot fully determine the outcome. In his general conference talk in 1972, President Harold B. Lee shared President McKay's quote but added, "No home is a failure as long as that home doesn't give up."[71] Clearly, effort matters. Elder Carmack also cautioned parents not to punish themselves because of the concepts embodied in the quote. He clarified, "Because this statement was intended to inspire parents to become or stay involved with their children, it should not be taken to mean that parents who have indeed put great time, effort, and sacrifice into parenting, and yet who have still not reaped the desired rewards, have failed."[72]

Celebrating other life successes in spite of family disappointments also seems like a healthy strategy. One father I interviewed pointed out that even though he felt his track record of keeping children in the Church was not perfect, he appreciated that, in the rest of his professional life, he had been able to make some useful contributions. "I had lots of other successes in my life. I know that no success can compensate for failure in the home and other successes can never override this. But in some ways, it sort of worked as a payback. If some of my other endeavors make a difference, it made me feel I was on the right track. And it helps me to feel I'm not a complete failure because I've done well in my profession and in the community. In total, things went well in my life."

This father also felt great happiness that he was still close to his children and that they shared a warm bond of love and appreciation. Other successes may not fully compensate, but they do help take some of the sting out of our children's actions. It's okay to celebrate them!

Serving Others

Many of those I interviewed discovered that serving others was a particularly powerful way to find healing in the midst of disappointment over children's choices. One mother of three non-attending teenagers found that her feelings of failure were most distressing while she was attending church until she realized that church was the perfect place to serve others. She said,

> One Sunday, I so did not want to go to church. I got thinking, *I have got to figure out how I can continue to* want *to go to church, even though it isn't always a comfortable place to be.* I remember the one theme that stuck out was, 'Who can I serve? How can I contribute?' I knew I had to stop thinking about how upsetting this was for me. I realized that you could completely change how you feel about something by how you think about it. I wrote about this day in my journal; it was an epiphany for me. I knew I needed a reason to go to church, and I decided that reason was to serve people. So I started going and looking around me and asking, 'Who looks like they could use someone to talk to?' I tried to go and *not* think, *How is this going to hurt me?* I tried to think instead, *Why might they have said that?* I started to think, *This person has tried really hard to prepare their talk, and they're really risking themselves by trying to speak and just be honest. I admire that in them.* In some ways, it doesn't matter what they say. I just looked at talks like that and marveled at how vulnerable people would be. I decided to just be grateful.

Some parents whose children have left the Church have found it healing to help other people's children when their own are in resistance mode. One mother I interviewed found it was balm to her soul to drive some Primary kids to church whose parents were completely inactive. She said with a smile, "I got to sit with them at church and tell them when they could and couldn't go out for a drink of water." The irony of the situation did not escape her.

Another couple in a similar situation was given the opportunity to assist a teenager in their congregation who was going through a rebellious phase. When their own children weren't listening to them, she and her husband loved being able to "wrap their arms around someone else's kid and have an impact on his life." They took this young man under their wing, invited him to family dinners and firesides where they were speaking, and just listened to him. When this young man's parents were at the end of their rope, this couple was able to fill in the gaps. The young man later called to announce that he had received his mission call and wanted these "extra parents" to come through the temple with him for the first time. The mother in this couple shared, "It was a gift of grace for me to be involved. His mother was so grateful to us, and she gave us lots of credit we did not deserve." And while they were all in the temple together, she felt a welcome spiritual reminder that someday this too would happen for her own children.

In my own life, I have found service for those outside my family to be a source of affirmation when my parenting efforts have fallen short. One of the great gifts I have been given is a Church calling to help youth from inner-city backgrounds get into college. In this unusual calling, I basically have the opportunity to help these young people in ways their parents would if they could. I encourage them in their schoolwork; suggest places to apply to college; help them with applications, housing, and financial aid; push them to make deadlines; and talk them through how to navigate the system. As a result, I have been blessed to see some success stories of young people going to Church colleges they would not have considered otherwise. I have seen some go on missions, find good spouses, and build strong marriages inside the Church. It's heartening to think I have played a small role in their lives. I'm grateful for notes like the one I received from one father: "Thank you so much for how you have loved my children. You have little idea how much impact you've had on my family's future."

Share Your Story When Appropriate

Another action step that can be a great service to others—and healing to oneself—is to share your struggles with others. We live in a culture where we are all trying so hard to do the right thing that it can be difficult to know when it's appropriate to admit we are falling short.

Sometimes we think we're the only ones struggling, and it can be challenging when we feel alone. Sharing your story can be a lifeline for those who are trying to succeed and need to know that others have also been in their shoes. One father admitted that he really appreciated hearing from speakers who had struggling children: "I appreciated those who could understand others who were trying their best and still lose out with their kids."

It's uncomfortable to tell people that your children are inactive, and there's no need for that to be the first descriptor out of your mouth when people ask about your children. But neither does that fact need to be buried all the time. Perhaps the person you talk to will be able to say just the thing you need to hear.

One mother told me that by speaking up about her daughter's disappointing decisions, she had an important conversation that gave her just the insight she needed to hear at that moment. Sometimes we just need to know that other people are not perfect. As one interviewee said, "Do you want to be friends with someone who appears perfect all the time? That would be a tough friend to have! If they were always perfect, would we trust them? Would they be real?" Baring your soul to some extent allows you to be that real friend who can actually provide support and comfort to others. Of course, it is important to be selective about when and where to share experiences.

Demonstrate Your Acceptance

It's also important for parents to celebrate the achievements of both non-LDS and LDS children as worthy and acceptable. One woman wrote about what happened to her after she quit going to church at eighteen. In her large LDS family, missions were celebrated in a fairly visible way. On the wall in her grandmother's living room wall were the photographs of all the young men in the family who had served missions, along with the flag for each country in which they had served. As she described it, this missionary wall was located in the epicenter of their family's world, and was "a sacred wall seen by all who visit."[73]

This wall mattered a great deal to her family, but because this woman had left the Church, she recognized it didn't matter what good she did in the world, she would still never make it onto that wall.

Then, at thirty, she decided to serve in the Peace Corps. She went on a journey to Madagascar and discovered new vistas of meaning in her worldview. She said of the experience, "I lost myself." Partway through her Peace Corps experience, she learned that her grandmother had broken all the rules and put up *her* photo and flag on the missionary wall along with all of her relatives who had served missions. When she returned home to visit, it was an emotional moment for them when her grandmother explained, "Service is service."[74] Whether there is a missionary wall in our homes or not, we can look for ways to demonstrate acceptance for all our children, both those in or out of the Church fold.

Chapter 8

What Works: Hold onto Hope

Hope is the thing with feathers
That perches in the soul,
And sings the tune without the words,
And never stops at all.[75]

—Emily Dickinson

Parents with daughters and sons who no longer participate in the gospel face a mental challenge: fully accepting their children as they are, yet still hoping for the miracle that they may someday change and return to full fellowship and a gospel-oriented life. Keeping both concepts balanced is tricky—a bit like applying for your dream job knowing the odds are against you, but nevertheless throwing your hat in the ring and hoping your résumé will be the one to rise to the top of the pile. After all, *someone* has to land those top jobs. And I will be the first to encourage people to hang onto that hope.

We have all heard experiences of people returning to full activity in the Church or converting later in life after a period of wandering from gospel paths. These stories are a lifeline because they remind us that such things can also happen for our children.

One mother found that hope was what got her through her son's period of agnosticism and soul-searching before he eventually decided to go on a mission. During this time, she found it helpful to write the word *hope* over and over in her journal, almost mantra-like. She clung to the concept, and her son eventually returned in time to serve a mission. She wrote the following:

> The message of hope is essential when you are in the middle of pain. And my sense of hope came from the realization that part of my pain was a sense of guilt and failure on my part. As I was examining—once again—all the things I had done wrong and how much I had failed as a mother, the merciful thought—which felt like it came directly from God—entered my mind, which was, *He is NOT your child. I loaned him to you. I love him even more than you and I'm not feeling like a failure or feeling guilty about him or any of my other wandering children.* And from that moment on, I stopped feeling guilty and began to focus on what a lovely child of God he was and that because I knew God loved him even more than I did, I could have hope.

She pointed out that even though things did work out for her in her family, the interim pain of the experience of watching her son wander untethered to gospel teachings was still real and difficult.

One of the most remarkable scriptural examples of a wandering child who later returns to a full-fledged gospel lifestyle comes from the Book of Mormon. Alma's rebellious son, Alma the Younger, was a rascal—so articulate and charismatic that he convinced many to follow him into idolatry and iniquity. He was such a successful champion for evil that his actions threatened the existence of the Church. His father offered many prayers on his behalf, and finally these prayers were miraculously and memorably answered. Talk about divine intervention! Down from the clouds came an angel so powerful that the earth shook, and Alma was left essentially comatose, unable to speak or move. After two days, Alma came back to his senses a changed man. From then on, he used his remarkable powers of persuasion to help people and build up the Church.

Most conversion stories do *not* involve angels, as did Alma's, but they can seem no less miraculous. I remember walking into the San Diego California Temple one day to see my former boss, all dressed in white, now a temple worker. I was dumbfounded and had to do a double take. Prior to this, my most vivid memory of this man was watching him walk down the hallway of the law firm, carrying a cup of coffee. For thirty years, he had refused to join the Church during his children's youth. But one day, he decided he wanted what he saw his LDS son bringing to the table as a new father. Something inside his soul shifted, and he was ready for conversion.

Later-life conversions happen outside the Church as well. USC professor Vern Bengston became interested in faith when he was sixty-seven years old, long after his own children were raised. All his life, he had rejected his mother's nudges toward religion, and she had given up on him. But an urge led him into a church building in Santa Barbara on Easter Sunday. He said, "It was a Gothic-looking church, and [I] entered a bit late, after the service had started." When he arrived, "the organ was roaring, the congregation was singing, the pillars were going up to heaven, the light was sifting down through the stained glass windows. I was just overwhelmed. I found my way to a pew and started crying. . . . I haven't been the same since."[76] Since then, he has studied and written about how families pass along faith through the generations. He's actively involved in his local congregation, and to this day he urges, "Don't give up on the prodigals, because many do return."[77]

Happily for some parents, many prodigals return while young. Researcher Stan Albrecht found that there is a good chance people will return to church after departing in their late teens or early twenties. In fact, he found "a clear majority of those who leave come back."[78] For many young people, these forays down rebellious paths are brief. One interviewee shared that her daughter spent some years during college living a different lifestyle, but eventually she wanted to return. For her, the pull of family was simply so strong that she didn't want to be the only one missing out on that connection.

A *New York Times* article described the experience of a young LDS student in the BYU animation department who had a similar change of heart while young. He led what he called a relatively "undisciplined life" as a teen in rural Idaho, socializing with other students who were not a good influence on him, and lying about his whereabouts to his parents. During college, he discovered he wanted more than anything "to be a really good person." He said, "That thought just hit me like a ton of bricks." He went on a mission and made it his goal to do good in the world. The author of the article pointed out, "It was the reverse of the typical coming-of-age-at-college story: he felt liberated enough to experiment, so he experimented with returning to the values he was raised with."[79]

Another returning prodigal story in the *Ensign* tells of a young man who was smoking, drinking, and doing drugs by sixteen. He dropped out of school and moved in with his girlfriend. His parents rarely saw him, but they prayed for him constantly. Then one day, he came back home with a new outlook on life. He had encountered a girl at a party who quizzed him about his LDS beliefs. "Before he could tell her he no longer knew the answers, words started coming out of his mouth. He found himself answering her questions as fast as she asked them. He said he did not remember having learned the things he spoke, but he knew his words were true. He wondered why he was living as he was when he still believed the gospel. After three days of soul-searching, he decided to leave behind the life he had been leading. He had come home to ask for help in starting over." Through a supportive family, a loving bishop, and the blessing of finding an active LDS woman to marry in the temple, this young man made a full return to the Church.[80]

In the April 2015 general conference, Elder Brent H. Nielson shared the story of his sister, Susan, who left the Church later in life—after being married in the temple—to the consternation of the rest of the family. Through the ensuing years, his family chose to follow the example of the father of the prodigal son, who "had to figuratively let her go—but not without her knowing and feeling our sincere love for her." They continued to reach out to her, inviting her to important family events, and attending her important life events as well. After many years, Elder Nielson was prompted by his wife to invite Susan to watch the session of general conference in which he was sustained as a new General Authority. He stated, "During this and other unique heaven-sent experiences, my sister—like the prodigal son—came to herself (see Luke 15:17). The words of prophets and apostles and the love of her family moved her to turn and begin the walk back home. After 15 years our daughter and sister who was lost had been found. The watch and the wait were over."[81]

Stories like these help people believe that miracles can also occur in their own families. One mother I interviewed suggested that parents let go of preconceived notions of exactly how these miracles will take place. She encouraged people to consider that miracles can happen in ways we can't even imagine, but that we also need to manage our expectations. As she said, "It's probably pretty unlikely for kids to show up at the front door and say, 'I'm back and I want to go on a mission now.' But just because it doesn't happen that way doesn't mean God's hand is not there."

If we are only willing to accept a miracle as something that happens a certain way, we may shut ourselves off and limit our view. We might miss that something even better is happening. Perhaps the miracle we should hope for is that our children will learn some important lessons that will make them better, healthier, happier people. If we can see the hand of God nudging them in a positive direction, even if they aren't fully back, this too can be a miracle. There is a great deal of evidence that God takes us where we are and prods us in directions that will help us, so long as we are willing to listen and learn.

Prophetic Assurances

Another source of great comfort and hope comes from the words of prophets and Apostles, which reassure parents that their obedience will help keep children sealed to them. Our Church doctrine teaches that God's laws are fair and just, and that we all must walk our own path back to God. The Articles of Faith clearly spell out, "We believe that men will be punished for their own sins, and not for Adam's transgression" (Articles of Faith 1:2). Similarly, just as Adam's righteousness cannot save us, neither can a parent's righteousness be the deciding factor in a child's salvation. We know the demands of justice must be met, but we can also enjoy a strong hope for the blessing of mercy. There is great comfort in the idea presented by both Elder Quentin L. Cook and Elder Mark E. Peterson—and quoted by one parent I interviewed: "To believe in God is to know that all the rules are fair, and there will be wonderful surprises."[82]

Many Church leaders have made positive, hopeful statements regarding what will happen with our wayward children. In each case, the prophetic counsel is to keep faith and hope for their eventual return. One of my interviewees shared that President Uchtdorf recently assured a group of temple workers in Salt Lake that not one of their wayward children would be lost. He quoted from a talk given by Orson Whitney in the April 1929 general conference that highlights the powerful influence of the Savior in making this promise come true:

> You parents of the wilful and the wayward! Don't give them up. Don't cast them off. They are not utterly lost. The Shepherd will find his sheep. They were his before they were yours—long before he entrusted them to your care; and you cannot begin to love them as he loves them. They have but strayed in ignorance from the Path of Right, and God is merciful to ignorance. Only the fulness of knowledge brings the fulness of accountability. Our Heavenly Father is far more merciful, infinitely more charitable, than even the best of his servants, and the Everlasting Gospel is mightier in power to save than our narrow finite minds can comprehend.[83]

I love the optimism embedded in that statement. It's reassuring to understand that one reason our children stray is due to their ignorance of gospel principles, not simply because of willful disobedience. I love believing that when our children have a more complete understanding of the gospel, they too will be newly converted in ways they currently are not. The hope of God's mercy is something to cling to.

Of course, the demands of justice must also be met, as Elder Bednar pointed out when he said, "Ultimately, a child must exercise his or her moral agency and respond in faith, repent with full purpose of heart, and act in accordance with the teachings of Christ."[84] Orson Whitney acknowledged this too when he said that wayward children will eventually feel motivated to "pay their debt to justice" and "suffer for their sins."[85] Yet it's a great blessing to know that children will eventually feel the pull of the Savior who cares about them infinitely more than we can imagine.

Other prophets have made similar statements of reassurance and hope. As long as we continue working hard to show our children the way, we can feel confident that they will eventually find their way back to the path and enjoy its blessings. Lorenzo Snow stated:

> If you succeed in passing through these trials and afflictions and receive a resurrection, you will, by the power of the Priesthood, work and labor, as the Son of God has, until you get all your sons and

> daughters in the path of exaltation and glory. This is just as sure as that the sun rose this morning over yonder mountains. Therefore, mourn not because all your sons and daughters do not follow in the path that you have marked out to them, or give heed to your counsels. Inasmuch as we succeed in securing eternal glory, and stand as saviors, and as kings and priests to our God, we will save our posterity.[86]

What a wonderful thought! The demands of justice must be met, but we can hold onto the promise of eventual mercy and our children's eventual reconciliation to the gospel path.

Two points may help clarify how both the demands of mercy and justice can be met. First, we need to keep in mind the timeline of the Lord. We're promised that our children will return, but we do not know exactly when this will be happening. We do not know if it will be in this lifetime or the next, or even when in the next life.

As Orson Whitney taught, "Though some of the sheep may wander, the eye of the Shepherd is upon them, and sooner or later they will feel the tentacles of Divine Providence reaching out after them and drawing them back to the fold. Either in this life or the life to come, they will return."[87]

Brigham Young also affirmed that when parents continually strive to do good, children "are bound up to their parents by an everlasting tie, and no power of earth or hell can separate them from their parents in eternity."[88]

As the timeline of the Lord stretches into eternity, the demands of justice will be resolved in ways we don't yet understand. But it's nice to know that we do have a lifetime and beyond to work these things out.

A second point of clarification is that Church leaders corroborate that parents can't be held responsible for all the variables and circumstances that impact children's choices. Elder Boyd K. Packer assured that in an ideal world with better information, of course children would choose a spiritual path back to God. As he said, "The measure of our success as parents . . . will not rest solely on how our children turn out. That judgment would be just only if we could raise our families in a perfectly moral environment, and that now is not possible." He expressed great sympathy and reassurance for parents in this situation: "It is not uncommon for responsible parents to lose one of their children, for a time, to influences over which they have no control. They agonize over rebellious sons or daughters. They are puzzled over why they are so helpless when they have tried so hard to do what they should. It is my conviction that those wicked influences one day will be overruled."[89] Parents may continually strive to give children the whole picture so they can choose wisely, but only God can entirely accomplish this, and on His own timeline. It's up to us to be patient, keep on striving to do our best, and forgive ourselves for factors over which we have no control.

This prophetic counsel gives us great reason to believe that, in the end, all of God's rules will be equitable, but perhaps through some surprising mechanisms, our children may yet return to the fold. While this detour may not be what we would choose for them or ourselves, we can rest a little more peacefully at night knowing that God loves our children more than we do, He wants their success even more than we do, His timeline is long, and we do not understand all the mechanisms by which our children can eventually return. In the meantime, it's up to us to live righteous lives and believe in the possibility of a miraculous return for them.

Keep the Long View

Some people have set good examples for keeping this perspective of hope. One father shared that he refused to think negatively about the future. He said he had done his best to get educated about how to help his struggling son, but he didn't pretend to know what will happen. He said, "The story is not written yet." A mother suggested, "I think you just show your children how happy the gospel makes you in your life. They will see that and come around eventually."

For her, this is exactly what happened. She shared,

> One of my daughters was always the one who had the most chance of being rebellious. When she started dating her future husband, and it was clear they were considering marriage, she came to me and asked, "Do you think it would be okay if we found a nice Protestant church we could start attending together?" I told her, "Sure, that's fine, but just be aware of all the things you would be giving up, including Primary, Young Women's, Young Men's, visiting teaching, home teaching, service, and a community like ours.

> After they married, I heard that the missionaries were scheduled to come talk to her husband to help clarify what ideologies our daughter had grown up with. Then we got word that her husband had decided to join the Church. A year later, they went through the temple. Now he was just called to be the Gospel Doctrine class teacher. So you never know. The story isn't over until it's over.

President Uchtdorf suggested that sometimes we get in trouble when we believe that the end of the story has already been written, when in reality we are only in the middle.[90] We still get to write the end of the story, and where we are can be a beautiful beginning.

As we work to make this story turn out well, we can benefit from the advice of a wise psychologist about how to interact with those who have departed. His suggestions were: "Remember that you don't have to operate from a place of fear or anger or hatred or suspicion. You can operate from a place of faith and hope and love, knowing that this is all part of God's eternal plan. In the afterlife, it's going to be worked out. Trust in your heavenly parents that things are going to work out."[91] And as Elder John Carmack urged, "Never give up. If you cannot seem to reach your daughter or son now, you can at least keep trying and keep loving them. . . . Be strong and courageous. You will see it through."[92]

Chapter 9

Conclusion: Balancing Pain and Joy

There's no question that making peace with children's faith transitions is a daunting challenge. One mother expressed this pain poignantly when she told her adult daughter that having two children leave the Church was harder for her than having two of her babies die in their first year of life.

Another parent of an inactive daughter shared that it would have been easier for her in some ways if her daughter were sick or dying. "Everyone would rally to my side and do whatever they could. When your daughter has become inactive, you don't even dare tell people." I interviewed one mom who was a social worker. She had raised nine children and faced issues with homosexuality, drug abuse, pregnancy outside marriage, and everything else "except suicide," she said. When I told her I was doing research on how parents find peace with their children's choices, her response was, "What makes you think they *do* find peace?"

Such comments give some idea just how difficult it is to come to a full resolution after a child has gone AWOL from the gospel path. For those I interviewed, feelings of pain resurface cyclically. One father expressed to me, "This never goes away. Sometimes I'll start thinking about it again. Some of my thoughts are positive, and sometimes not."

But my research has helped me feel that there are some important tools available to assist people in getting through the times when negative thoughts threaten parents' equilibrium. I have attempted to offer a wide range of ideas to help people think and act in ways that will bring them some solace and strength. It is my hope that something I have shared will help people move in positive, helpful directions. At the least, my goal has been to help others feel less alone with this burden. In addition to all of the extremely helpful gospel scaffolding such as scriptures, church and temple attendance, and prayer, it can also be heartening to just listen to people who have blazed the trail. The thoughts and actions that have brought them comfort may also be a source of comfort for others.

One thing my interviewees all had in common was a great love of the gospel and an appreciation for its role in their lives. One father described an experience he had many years ago as he stood in the Salt Lake Tabernacle with his wife and realized, "This place is our place. These are our people. Don't ask me why, but this is true. Eventually, it's a choice, and this is our choice. I choose it, and I choose it again tomorrow, and the next day. The gospel is tied up in this one powerful, beautiful, true thing for me."

The gospel is also a wonderful, joyful blessing in my own life. Being a member of The Church of Jesus Christ of Latter-day Saints is soul-stretching and affirming. The gospel rings true for me. The scriptures we have are "virtuous, lovely, . . . of good report [and] praiseworthy" (Articles of Faith 1:13). I appreciate the opportunities I have to serve my fellow Saints and to embrace the spiritual nudges I feel when hearing their stories. I recognize the blessing it is for me to have been born into this family of Saints. I appreciate that living the gospel makes my life easier, not harder. As one of my interviewees expressed, "The older I get, the more I recognize that what the gospel and the Church ask of me are what I *want* required of me."

These feelings of love for the gospel truths and lifestyle are powerful and soul-sustaining. They make people want to share their joy—and that much harder for them when children resist. Nevertheless, it's possible to experience this joy *simultaneously* with its attendant pain. Paul expressed this beautifully in a letter to the Philippians: "I have learned, in whatsoever state I am, therewith to be content. I know both how to be abased, and I know how to abound: every where and in all things I am instructed both to be full and to be hungry, both to abound and to suffer need. I can do all things through Christ which strengtheneth me" (Philippians 4:11–13). The mother who shared this scripture with me said that she has learned over time to be "full of pain and full of joy simultaneously, or to at least be aware of both at the same time." She then said, "I think a whole person can have whole pain and whole happiness at the same time." This is a magical goal, one that has the power to transform. We don't need to completely eradicate our pain, but rather learn to live with it in balance with our joy.

In fact, many sorrows bring accompanying joys. One of the blessings of having children who are no longer participating in the Church is that we gain a much greater appreciation for the struggles of others. We have an opportunity to reach out and bless them, and we become more sensitive to what will help or hurt others. As one mom said, "I now know the things I should *not* say." She admitted with remarkable candor that she "would happily give up any sensitivity I have gained to have all my kids in church and be able to say things that hurt other people's feelings." But in the end, she appreciates the gift of being able to empathize with others. As she said, "It's not what I would choose, but maybe there's a role I can play, some help I can give someone else. My friend's words to me have helped me. These things are valuable, and I have to be grateful for that."

Anytime we experience adversity, we gain the potential to stretch and transform into better people. President Thomas S. Monson expressed this well when he said,

> We know that there are times when we will experience heartbreaking sorrow, when we will grieve, and when we may be tested to our limits. However, such difficulties allow us to change for the better, to rebuild our lives in the way our Heavenly Father teaches us, and to become something different from what we were—better than we were, more understanding than we were, more empathetic than we were, with stronger testimonies than we had before.[93]

As we live out the story of our lives, it's helpful to remember that we do not know what will happen to our children. God's reckoning of time is vastly different from ours, and we do not know the end of their stories. If we did know that our children would eventually return, would that change how we act in our stories today? I believe we might live them with a greater degree of peace, love, and acceptance for our current reality.

In the end, living our lives with a sense of peace comes down to a matter of faith. Heavenly Father has our children in His watchful care. He loves them, and He knows them much better than we do. He will do everything He can to help them become the best people they can be.

And people do return. Recently, a woman in our stake spoke about how she returned to Church activity after fifteen years of absence. "Now," she said, "I am glad my self-exile is over; it was a cold and lonely way to live." She said she was grateful that "Jesus waited with open arms and great love" for her to "step onto the Comeback Trail and follow the road home."[94] While we wait for our children to find that eventual "Comeback Trail," or take their own paths in other directions, I hope we may all enjoy the journey and find the peace we seek.

Endnotes

1. Elizabeth Stone, "A Quote by Elizabeth Stone," *Goodreads.*
2. Dieter F. Uchtdorf, "A Matter of a Few Degrees," *Ensign*, May 2008.
3. Virginia Pearce, "Prayer: A Small and Simple Thing," BYU Continuing Education, April 28, 2011, 4–5.
4. Ibid.
5. Ibid.
6. Cambridge University, Massachusetts, unpublished stake statistics (2014).
7. David Kinnaman and Aly Hawkins, *You Lost Me: Why Young Christians Are Leaving Church—and Rethinking Faith* (Grand Rapids, Michigan: Baker, 2011), 22.
8. Ibid., 23.
9. "America's Changing Religious Landscape," *Pew Research Centers Religion Public Life Project RSS*, May 11, 2015.
10. Kristen Moulton, "Christianity Shrinking in U.S.; Mormon Numbers Essentially Flat," *The Salt Lake Tribune,* May 12, 2015.
11. Vern L. Bengtson, Norella M. Putney, and Susan Harris, *Families and Faith: How Religion Is Passed Down Across Generations* (New York: Oxford University Press, 2013), 11, 59.

12. Quentin L. Cook, "The Lord Is My Light," *Ensign,* May 2015, 66.
13. Matthew Brown, "Passing the Torch: How Belief Passes from One Generation to the Next," *Deseret News,* February 2014, 11.
14. Peter Henderson and Kristina Cooke, "Special Report: Mormonism Besieged by the Modern Age," *Reuters.com,* January 31, 2012.
15. Kara E. Powell and Chap Clark, *StickyFaith: Everyday Ideas to Build Lasting Faith in Your Kids* (Grand Rapids: Michigan, Zondervan, 2011), 19.
16. "Open Up!" Boston stake singles conference program, October 11–13, 2013.
17. E. Jay Richardson, "Carving a Place for Those Who Wrestle with Their Testimony," fireside talk, given in Alberta, Canada, July 2013.
18. Terryl L. Givens, "Letter to a Doubter," *Interpreter: A Journal of Mormon Scripture,* April 2013.
19. Jack Zenger, talk on dealing with doubters, given in Midway, Utah, September 22, 2013.
20. Robert A. Rees, *Why I Stay: The Challenges of Discipleship for Contemporary Mormons* (Salt Lake City: Signature, 2011).
21. Eugene England, *Why the Church Is as True as the Gospel* (Salt Lake City: Bookcraft, 1986).
22. "Understanding Mormon Disbelief Survey—March 2012 Results and Analysis." *Why Mormons Question: Seeking to Better Understand Why Some Mormons Struggle to Believe in Mormonism,* May 21, 2012.
23. Jeffrey Arnett and Elizabeth Fishel, *When Will My Grown-up Kid Grow Up?: Loving and Understanding Your Emerging Adult* (New York: Workman, 2013), 231.
24. "'Nones' on the Rise," *Pew Research Centers Religion Public Life Project RSS,* Pew Research Center, October 9, 2012.
25. Ibid.
26. Vern L. Bengtson, *Families and Faith,* 52.
27. Ibid.
28. Christian Smith and Patricia Snell, *Souls in Transition: The Religious and Spiritual Lives of Emerging Adults* (Oxford: Oxford University Press, 2009).

29. Jeffrey Arnett, *When Will My Grown-up Kid Grow Up?*, 233–34.
30. Vern L. Bengtson, *Families and Faith,* 8.
31. Jason DeParle and Sabrina Tavernise, "For Women Under 30, Most Births Occur Outside Marriage," *New York Times,* February 17, 2012.
32. Andrea Caumont, "More of Today's Single Mothers Have Never Been Married," *Pew Research Center RSS*, August 16, 2013, 1.
33. Jodi Kantor and Laurie Goodstein, "From Mormon Women, a Flood of Requests and Questions on Their Role in the Church," *New York Times,* March 6, 2014.
34. Neylan McBaine, "To Do the Business of the Church: A Cooperative Paradigm for Examining Gendered Participation Within Church Organizational Structure," *FAIR Journal*, September 18, 2013, 3.
35. Peggy Fletcher Stack, "'Sister Missionaries' Causing a Gender Shift in Mormonism, BYU Professor Says," *Salt Lake Tribune* March 27, 2014.
36. E. Jay Richardson, "Carving a Place," 3.
37. John Branch, "NFL Prospect Michael Sam Proudly Says What Teammates Knew: He's Gay," *New York Times,* February 9, 2014.
38. "Global Views on Morality," *Pew Research Centers Global Attitudes Project RSS*, Pew Research Center, 2007.
39. Jeffrey Arnett, *When Will My Grown-up Kid Grow Up?*, 243.
40. E. Jay Richardson, "Carving a Place," 2.
41. Jeffrey Arnett, *When Will My Grown-up Kid Grow Up?*, 230.
42. Stan L. Albrecht, "The Consequential Dimension of Mormon Religiosity," *Latter-day Saint Social Life: Social Research on the LDS Church and Its Members* (Provo, Utah: Religious Studies Center, 1998), 253–92.
43. Matthew Brown, "Passing the Torch," 11.
44. Marian S. Bergin, "As Parents, What Do We Do with the Pain?" *Women of Wisdom & Knowledge: Talks Selected from the BYU Women's Conferences* (Salt Lake City: Deseret Book, 1990), 153–58.
45. Vern L. Bengtson, *Families and Faith*, 72.

46. Jeffrey Arnett, *When Will My Grown-up Kid Grow Up?,* 231.
47. Amy Chua and Jed Rubenfeld, "What Drives Success?," *New York Times,* January 25, 2014.
48. Robert Kirby, "How Much Pain Does Your Faith Cause?," *Salt Lake Tribune,* July 12, 2014.
49. John K. Carmack, "When Our Children Go Astray," *Ensign,* February 1997.
50. Byron Katie and Stephen Mitchell, *Loving What Is: Four Questions That Can Change Your Life* (New York: Harmony, 2002).
51. John K. Carmack, "When Our Children Go Astray."
52. Carlfred Broderick, *The Uses of Adversity* (Salt Lake City: Deseret Book, 2008), chapter 12.
53. Ibid.
54. *Journal of Discourses,* 26 vols. (London: Latter-day Saints' Book Depot, 1854), 2:301.
55. Yann Martel, *Life of Pi: A Novel* (New York: Harcourt, 2001).
56. Terryl L. Givens, "Letter to a Doubter," *Interpreter: A Journal of Mormon Scripture,* April 2013.
57. Sean McDowell; as quoted in David Kinnaman, *You Lost Me,* 241–2.
58. Ibid.
59. Dieter F. Uchtdorf, "The Merciful Obtain Mercy," *Ensign,* May 2012.
60. John K. Carmack, "When Our Children Go Astray."
61. Jeffrey Arnett, *When Will My Grown-up Kid Grow Up?,* 239–40.
62. Ibid., 240.
63. John A. Widtsoe, "Temple Worship," *Utah Genealogical and Historical Magazine,* April 1921: 63–64; as quoted by David B. Haight, *Ensign,* November 1990.
64. John K. Carmack, "When Our Children Go Astray."
65. E. Jay Richardson, "Carving a Place," 3.
66. Ibid., 5.

67. James E. Faust, "Continuous Revelation," *Ensign,* November 1989.

68. "David O. McKay—Quotes," *David O. McKay—Quotes*, Church history website, 2004.

69. John K. Carmack, "When Our Children Go Astray."

70. James E. McCulloch, *Home: The Savior of Civilization* (Washington, DC: Southern Co-operative League, 1924); as quoted in Conference Report, April 1935, 116.

71. Harold B. Lee, "Maintain Your Place as a Woman," *Ensign,* February 1972.

72. John K. Carmack, "When Our Children Go Astray."

73. Monica Yancey, "Mine Eyes Have Seen," *Salt Lake City Opinion,* February 12, 2014, 3.

74. Ibid.

75. Emily Dickinson, *The Complete Poems of Emily Dickinson* (Boston: Little Brown, 1960).

76. Vern L. Bengtson, *Families and Faith,* 1; as quoted in Matthew Brown, "Passing the Torch."

77. Vern L. Bengtson, *Families and Faith*, 197.

78. Stan L. Albrecht, "The Consequential Dimension of Mormon Religiosity," 13.

79. Jon Mooallem, "When Hollywood Wants Good, Clean Fun, It Goes to Mormon Country," *New York Times,* May 23, 2013.

80. "Would Matthew Return?" *Ensign*, October, 2013, 76.

81. Brent H. Van Nielson, "Waiting for the Prodigal," *Ensign,* May 2015, 103.

82. Marion D. Hanks, "A Loving, Communicating God," *Ensign,* October 1992.

83. Orson F. Whitney, in Conference Report, April 1921, 110.

84. David A. Bednar, "Faithful Parents and Wayward Children: Sustaining Hope While Overcoming Misunderstanding," *Ensign,* March 2014, 31.

85. Orson F. Whitney, in Conference Report, April 1921, 110.

86. Lorenzo Snow; as quoted in "Hope for Parents of Wayward Children," *Ensign,* September 2002.
87. Orson F. Whitney, in Conference Report, April 1921, 110.
88. Brigham Young; as quoted in "Hope for Parents of Wayward Children," *Ensign,* September 2002.
89. Boyd K. Packer, "Our Moral Environment," *Ensign,* May 1992, 68.
90. Dieter F. Uchtdorf, "Grateful in Any Circumstances," *Ensign,* May 2014.
91. John Dehlin, "Top 5 Myths and Truths About Why Committed Mormons Leave the Church," *Mormonstories.org,* June 12, 2014.
92. John K. Carmack, "When Our Children Go Astray."
93. Thomas S. Monson, "I Will Not Fail Thee, nor Forsake Thee," *Ensign,* November 2013.
94. Deborah S. Butler, "Reaching Out to Others," talk given in Arlington, Massachusetts, February 2014.

About the Author

Robin Zenger Baker has been lucky enough to raise four wonderful children with her husband in the Boston area. For fun, she enjoys bird-watching, boogie boarding, and helping inner city Boston teens get into college. She has studied psychology and organizational behavior at Stanford, BYU, and UCLA and has taught organizational behavior at Boston University. She is currently studying marriage and family therapy at the University of Massachusetts Boston. In between her homework assignments, she enjoys dancing the chicken dance and reading stories with her adorable first granddaughter.

0 26575 16478 7